GRACE AND LAW
IN SECOND ISAIAH

'I am the Lord'

Philip B. Harner

Ancient Near Eastern Texts and Studies
Volume 2

The Edwin Mellen Press
Lewiston/Queenston

Library of Congress Cataloging-in-Publication Data

Harner, Philip B.
  Grace and law in Second Isaiah : 'I am the Lord' / Philip B. Harner.
  p. cm. -- (Ancient Near Eastern texts and studies ; v. 2)
  Bibliography: p.
  Includes index.
  ISBN 0-88946-087-6
  1. Bible. O.T. Isaiah XL-LV--Criticism, interpretation, etc.
2. Grace (Theology)--Biblical teaching.   3. Law (Theology)--Biblical
teaching.   I. Title.   II. Series.
BS1520.H37 1988
224'.106--dc19   87-22759
                                                                 CIP

BS
1520
.H37
1988

This is volume 2 in the continuing series
Ancient Near Eastern Texts and Studies
Volume 2 ISBN 0-88946-087-6
ANETS Series ISBN 0-88946-085-X

The Edwin Mellen Press   The Edwin Mellen Press
Box 450   Box 67
Lewiston, New York   Queenston, Ontario
USA 14092   L0S 1L0 CANADA

TABLE OF CONTENTS

PREFACE

This study presents the argument that II Isaiah proclaimed a message which included the themes of both "grace" and "law." He proclaimed a message of "grace" in assuring his fellow exiles in Babylon that Yahweh, their God, would soon come to their aid, set them free, and lead them home again. Yahweh's actions would be an expression of grace because he would act on the basis of his love and concern for his people, freely taking the initiative to intervene in their history and deliver them from captivity. II Isaiah also proclaimed a message of "law" in reminding the people that they still constituted the covenant community of Israel. They were to respond to God's grace by accepting the same kinds of covenant obligations that they had known throughout their history from the time of the covenant at Mt. Sinai. Further, they were to enlarge their understanding of covenant obligation by undertaking a role on the scene of world history. They were to become "a covenant to the people, a light to the nations," that Yahweh's salvation might reach "to the end of the earth" (Is. 42:6; 49:6). In these ways, therefore, II Isaiah proclaimed a "holistic" message that included the themes of both grace and law.

The present study differs from many other interpretations of II Isaiah in arguing that his message comprised both grace and law, rather than focusing on grace alone. A number of commentators understand the writings of II Isaiah as a wonderful, joyful message of salvation or deliverance from captivity, without any apparent concern for Israel's continuing role as a covenant community with ethical obligations of the kind represented by the Sinai

covenant. Claus Westermann, for example, remarks,
"The unique feature of the prophecy of Deutero-Isaiah
is this, the hour summoned him to the task of proclaiming salvation, and nothing but salvation, to his
people; at the same time, however, he wears the mantle
of the pre-exilic prophets of doom."[1] By relating II
Isaiah to the pre-exilic judgment prophets, Westermann
means that he regarded the fall of Jerusalem as the
fulfillment of the judgment predicted by these prophets.
In analyzing II Isaiah's message for his own time,
however, Westermann summarizes it in terms of
"salvation, and nothing but salvation."

     Closely related to the issue of "law" or
"covenant obligation" is the question whether II Isaiah
still included the religious and ethical responsibilities
of the Sinai covenant in his understanding of Israel as
the people of Yahweh, not only as these people had been
in the past but as they were in his own day and would
continue to be after their return to their homeland.
It is true that II Isaiah makes no explicit mention of
the Sinai covenant. Thus Walther Eichrodt can say,
"In common with earlier prophecy he has nothing to say
about the particular covenant at Sinai, but speaks
instead of the deliverance from Egypt, in which Yahweh
formed his people for himself."[2] Eichrodt is correct,
of course, in indicating that II Isaiah speaks of the
Exodus from Egypt, since the prophet often refers to
this event as the model par excellence for the new
deliverance that Yahweh will soon bring to the exiles
in Babylon. The particular question that must be
raised here is whether II Isaiah was still influenced
by the Sinai covenant in formulating his understanding
of Israel as the continuing people of Yahweh, even
though he does not mention this covenant directly.

Comments by James Muilenburg seem to reflect some
uncertainty concerning II Isaiah's attitude toward the
Sinai covenant, especially as it would have continuing
significance for Israel. Muilenburg says, for example,
of II Isaiah, "He has nothing to say of the Sinaitic
covenant, and his only allusion to a historical covenant
refers to David, the leader of the people (55:3-5)."[3]
Yet elsewhere Muilenburg writes as if II Isaiah's
perspective was indeed governed by the reality of the
Sinai covenant, and he himself provides Old Testament
references to the Sinai covenant in explaining certain
passages in II Isaiah's writings. Thus Muilenburg
remarks, in discussing the view of Yahweh as the Holy
One of Israel:

> Yahweh's holiness, while uniquely and
> peculiarly his, manifests itself in
> mighty acts and wonders, but supremely
> in the redemption of his people. Here,
> as elsewhere, the prophet is laying hold
> of the fundamental reality of Mosaic
> religion (cf. Exod. 19:5-6). Holiness
> demands responsibility, Israel is
> forever accountable to her holy Lord.[4]

In a similar vein Muilenburg suggests that II Isaiah
still regards Israel as the covenant people, even after
all her failures to live up to this role throughout her
history. Commenting on Is. 42:4, Muilenburg writes,
"Covenant (bᵉrîth) and teaching (tôrāh) belong together;
the covenant people have been entrusted with teaching
or law (cf. Exod. 19-24; etc.)."[5]

As an example of a somewhat different approach to
II Isaiah, John L. McKenzie argues that the primary
theme in II Isaiah is really the mission of Israel in
making Yahweh known to the nations of the world. Within

this context the prophet emphasizes the theme of
deliverance or salvation. At the same time, McKenzie
notes, II Isaiah speaks of such terms as "law" or
"righteousness" as these concepts are applicable to the
nations of the world and to Israel herself. McKenzie
writes, for instance:

> The dominant theme of Second Isaiah is
> not salvation, but the mission of Israel
> for which the nation is saved . . .
> Yahweh's revelation and righteousness
> will go forth as a light to peoples
> (li 4) . . . through Israel his holiness
> will be manifested, and the nations shall
> recognize that Yahweh alone is God . . .
> It is through Israel that the nations
> must learn the law and the cult of
> Yahweh. [6]

McKenzie touches on these themes again when he
remarks, "Israel must know and proclaim Yahweh primarily
as a God who saves . . . ."[7] In summarizing II Isaiah's
vision of a new Israel, restored to her homeland,
McKenzie mentions "the restoration of the city, the
return of the exiles, security in the covenant of
Yahweh, the righteousness the restored community should
exhibit."[8] Within the context of "mission" as the
"dominant theme" in II Isaiah, it is significant that
McKenzie identifies ideas such as "salvation" and
"righteousness" as essential themes in the proclamation
of II Isaiah. These themes correspond to the motifs of
"grace" and "law" with which the present study is
concerned. In recognizing the importance of both themes,
McKenzie places more emphasis than, for example,
Westermann, on the idea or law or covenant obligation
as an integral part of II Isaiah's proclamation.

These examples from recent studies of II Isaiah
illustrate the need for clarifying the role of law or
covenant obligation within the prophet's message to his
fellow exiles and his expectations for the future.
They raise the question to what extent II Isaiah proclaimed a message of "law" as well as "grace." In
particular, they point to the problem of the degree to
which the Sinai covenant entered into the texture of
the prophet's thought, since he makes no explicit
reference to this covenant. It would not seem necessary
to cite further commentators at this point, since these
issues, in the final analysis, must be addressed through
exegesis of the prophet's writings within their context
in Old Testament tradition. It is important, on the
other hand, to develop a methodology that will be
appropriate to the issues and to the writings of II
Isaiah.

This study presents the argument that II Isaiah
included the themes of both "grace" and "law" in his
message to his fellow exiles. To support this view,
the study first examines the meaning of the divine self-
predication "I am the Lord," or "I am Yahweh," as it
appears in a number of other Old Testament writings
which are, for the greater part, prior to II Isaiah.
The analysis of the formula in these sources indicates
that it was associated with both motifs, grace and law.
From its inception, and throughout Old Testament
tradition, the formula "I am Yahweh" had the function
of communicating the themes of grace and law,
continually reminding the people of Israel that Yahweh
was a God who acted graciously toward them and then
expected them to respond with faithful obedience to
their covenant obligations. Since II Isaiah frequently
employs the self-predication "I am Yahweh," the study

concludes that he also, like Old Testament tradition
generally, perceives the formula as a vehicle for
expressing and communicating the themes of grace and
law.

In this way the study seeks to bring together
two complexes of thought -- the meaning and function of
the formula "I am Yahweh," on the one hand, and the
analysis of the themes of grace and law in II Isaiah,
on the other. More specifically, the methodology of
the study rests on the concept of "warrant," the reason
or assumption which explains why a particular piece of
evidence can lead to an assertion. The following
example illustrates how the "warrant" can stand between
evidence and assertion:

> evidence: The cost of living is rising.
>
> warrant: Colleges are subject to
> increases in the cost of living.
>
> assertion: Colleges will face higher costs.

Frequently the warrant is not stated. This illustration,
for example, might be worded, "Because the cost of
living keeps rising, colleges will face higher costs."
Yet the warrant is implied even when it is not stated;
a rise in the cost of living would mean that colleges
face higher costs only if colleges are subject to
increases in the cost of living.

In terms of the present study, the evidence,
warrant, and assertion have the following forms:

> evidence: Throughout the pre-exilic
> period of Israelite history,
> the divine self-predication
> "I am Yahweh" was associated
> with the themes of both grace
> and law.
>
> warrant: Even after the destruction of

the temple and the fall of
Jerusalem, the Israelite people
would continue to associate the
formula "I am Yahweh" with both
themes.

assertion: When II Isaiah used "I am Yahweh"
in the exilic period, he would
associate it with both themes --
grace and law -- and would
assume that his audience would
also associate it with both of
these themes.

For this reason it would appear to be a legitimate
procedure to examine the meaning of the self-predication
"I am Yahweh" in Old Testament tradition, apart from II
Isaiah, and then argue that the phrase retained its
traditional connotations as II Isaiah himself used it.
The organization of the present study reflects this
procedure. After a brief introduction and survey of
extrabiblical parallels, the study analyzes the meaning
of the formula "I am Yahweh" in Old Testament sources
apart from II Isaiah. Then, in the light of this
analysis, it turns to II Isaiah himself and examines
his use of the formula. Although the concept of
"warrant" is valid, the study tries to avoid placing too
much weight upon it. The study does not simply assume
that II Isaiah used the formula in the same way as
previous tradition, but it seeks to find the meaning of
each example as II Isaiah used it in a particular
context. In addition to the formula "I am Yahweh,"
the study also analyzes two other formulas of self-
predication, "I am God" and "I am He." These occur
less frequently than "I am Yahweh," but they are
included for the sake of completeness. The study

concludes that II Isaiah did indeed employ formulas of divine self-predication as vehicles for communicating the themes of grace and law, even though a particular instance of a given formula did not always convey both of these themes.

CHAPTER I
Introduction

One of the most distinctive features of II
Isaiah's thought is his frequent use of several statements beginning with the words "I am," in which God
makes an assertion about himself that serves to state
his identity, describe his attributes, depict his
relationship to Israel, or summarize his activity.
Although these statements assume a number of different
forms, they involve basically three types of self-
predication: "I am Yahweh," "I am God," and "I am He."
Sometimes II Isaiah repeats the same statement within
a given passage (e.g., Is. 45:5-6); occasionally he
combines two forms of self-predication in the same
passage (e.g., Is. 41:4). In one instance he uses all
three types of self-predication within one passage
(Is. 43:8-13). From a stylistic point of view, II
Isaiah achieves variety of expression in several ways:
using different words for "I" or "God," adding
possessive suffixes ("I am your God"), and repeating
God's solemn, majestic "I" ("I, I am He"). All together,
statements of divine self-predication appear thirty times
throughout II Isaiah's writings.[9] Their repetitions,
combinations, variations, and frequency of use all
suggest that II Isaiah regarded self-predication as one
of the most important ways in which God turned to his
people and spoke to them in the form of direct address.

As it was indicated in the Preface, the purpose
of the present study is to analyze the background, form,
and function of these statements of divine self-
predication in II Isaiah, with special attention to the
question of the relationship between the themes of grace
and law. We may look first at similar assertions on the
part of gods or kings in other cultures of the ancient

Near East, as examples of the general rhetorical style
with which II Isaiah and his audience may have been
acquainted.   Then we may examine the use of "I am
Yahweh," "I am God," and "I am He" in Old Testament
writings apart from II Isaiah, so that we will be in a
better position to identify similarities or differences
between II Isaiah and other writers in their use of
these expressions.   Finally, we may look at II Isaiah's
own use of these three forms of self-predication, with
special attention to their relationship to one another,
the types of passages in which they appear, the ideas
or themes with which they are associated, and their
significance for an understanding of II Isaiah's
thought.

CHAPTER II
The "I Am" Style In The Ancient Near East

A number of examples from ancient literature suggest that the "I am" style of speaking, in which a god or a king identifies himself and describes his accomplishments, was rather widespread throughout the ancient Near East. In an Egyptian myth, for instance, the supreme god Re depicts himself as the creator of the world and then identifies himself with the three forms of deity in which the sun passes across the sky: "I am he who made heaven and earth, who knotted together the mountains, and created what is thereon . . . I am Khepri in the morning, Re at noon, and Atum who is in the evening."[10] This particular self-predication occurs in a myth in which the goddess Isis is questioning Re, trying to learn the secret name that is the source of his power. Although the text of the myth does not actually disclose this secret name, the story illustrates the importance of the concept of "name" in the ancient world as an indication of the inner reality and personal identity of a god or a human being.

The connection between Re and Atum appears also in an extract from the seventeenth chapter of the Book of the Dead, in which the creator-god Atum identifies himself, refers to the waters of chaos (Nun), and links himself with Re, the sun: "I am Atum when I was alone in Nun; I am Re in his (first) appearances, when he began to rule that which he had made . . . I am yesterday, while I know tomorrow."[11] In this passage Atum also associates himself with the "yesterday" of death and the "tomorrow" of rebirth, so that the thought of the passage moves from the creation of the world to the re-creation or rebirth of the individual

person into immortality. This movement of thought
suggests that the concept of the creation of the world,
at least in this particular self-predication, is
ancillary to the idea of individual immortality in which
the passage culminates. When we examine the self-
predications in II Isaiah, we will have the occasion to
ask in a similar way whether a particular idea, regardless of its importance in itself, is not stated
primarily because it establishes a basis for introducing
another idea that represents the major emphasis of the
passage.

In a third example from ancient Egyptian
literature, the self-predication of Harmakhis, the god
in the Sphinx, forms part of an oracle given to Thutmose
IV, who reigned about 1421-1413 B.C. In the oracle
Harmakhis promises to grant royal sovereignty to
Thutmose and asks him, in return, to clear away the
sand from the Sphinx:

> See me, look at me, my son, Thutmose!
> I am thy father, Harmakhis-Khepri-Re-Atum.
> I shall give thee my kingdom upon earth
> at the head of the living. Thou shalt
> wear the southern crown and the northern
> crown on the throne of Geb, the crown
> prince (of the gods) . . . The sands of
> the desert, that upon which I had been,
> were encroaching upon me; (but) I waited
> to let thee do what was in my heart . . .
> Behold, I am with thee; I am thy guide.[12]

In contrast to the previous examples that we have
examined, this self-predication introduces a specific
promise of assistance to the recipient of the oracle.
In this respect the passage is parallel to the salvation
oracle, a form of speech that II Isaiah employs very

effectively to communicate Yahweh's promise of help to
his people as they languish in exile (e.g., Is. 41:8-13,
14-16). The direct address to the recipient of the
oracle ("my son, Thutmose!") and the supporting clauses
of reassurance ("I am with thee; I am thy guide") also
provide parallels to the structure of the salvation
oracle in II Isaiah. Although there is no reason to
assume that Egyptian oracles were a direct source for
II Isaiah's own use of the salvation oracle, this
oracle is noteworthy because it does offer several
parallels to the form of the salvation oracle. In
particular, it illustrates the connection between divine
self-predication and the god's promise of help to the
recipient of the oracle. Rather unexpectedly, the
Egyptian oracle also includes a request or indirect
command (Thutmose is asked to clear away the encroaching
sands of the desert). In this way the passage touches
on the theme of human activity or responsibility, which
is not actually included in the salvation oracle in
II Isaiah.

    Some of the oracles delivered to kings in
ancient Syria and Assyria are even closer in form to
the salvation oracle as it appears in II Isaiah. In an
inscription from northern Syria in the eighth century
B.C., king Zakir uses the "I am" style to identify
himself, and then he quotes an oracle that he received
from his tutelary deity: "I am Zakir, king of Hamat and
Lu'ath. A humble man I am. Be'elshamayn [helped me]
and stood by me. Be'elshamayn made me king over
Hatarikka (Hadrach)." The king describes how, with the
help of his god Be'elshamayn, he defeated a coalition
of seven other kings ranged against him. In this
connection he quotes an oracle in which Be'elshamayn
assured him of his help: "Be'elshamayn [said to me]:

Do not fear, for I made you king, and I shall stand by
you to deliver you from all [these kings who] set up a
siege against you . . . ."[13] In this oracle the self-
predication of the deity is replaced by a narrative
introduction ("Be'elshamayn said to me"); in the same
way, II Isaiah sometimes replaces "I am Yahweh" with
"thus says Yahweh" near the beginning of a salvation
oracle (Is. 43:1; 44:2). Several other elements in the
Be'elshamayn oracle are directly parallel, at least in
a formal sense, to the salvation oracle in II Isaiah:
the phrase of reassurance ("do not fear"), the reference
to the god's previous action on behalf of the recipient
("for I made you king"), and the promise of future
deliverance ("and I shall stand by you . . .").

The self-predication of a divinity is prominent
in the Arbela oracles that were delivered to Esarhaddon,
king of Assyria from 680 to 669 B.C. Most of the oracles
were given in the name of the goddess Ishtar at the
cultic center of Arbela, although the gods Bel and Nabu
are also included as sources of one of the oracles. As
the following selection illustrates, the oracles deal
with the general theme of military victory:

> [Esarhad]don, king of the countries,
> fear not! . . . I am the great divine lady,
> I am the goddess Ishtar of Arbela, who
> will destroy your enemies from before
> your feet. What are the words of mine,
> which I spoke to you, that you did not
> rely upon? . . ."[14]

Formal parallels to the salvation oracle in II Isaiah
include the direct address to the recipient, the phrase
of reassurance ("fear not!"), the self-predication of
the divinity, the promise of help in the near future,
and the reference to support in the past. Oracles

concerning Ashurbanipal, king of Assyria from 668 to 633
B.C., also illustrate many of these parallels.[15] As in
the case of the Egyptian oracle given to Thutmose IV,
there would seem to be no reason to assume that these
oracles from Syria and Assyria had a direct influence
on II Isaiah's use of the salvation oracle. They do
derive, however, from times and areas that were rather
close to II Isaiah's own time and place (about 540 B.C.
in Babylon), and they also exhibit very close formal
parallels to the salvation oracle as II Isaiah uses it.
For these reasons the oracles from Syria and Assyria
may well illustrate a general oracular pattern with
which II Isaiah and his audience were acquainted.

In addition to divine self-predications, ancient
literature offers numerous examples in which a human
king uses the "I am" style of speaking. One of the
earliest of these may come from Sargon I, who established
the Akkadian empire about 2300 B.C.: "Sargon, the mighty
king, king of Agade, am I . . . ."[16] In the following
lines Sargon tells of his birth, his elevation to the
throne with the aid of the goddess Ishtar, and his many
accomplishments as king. Also very early, and much more
extensive, is the prologue to the Code of Hammurabi,
who probably reigned from 1728 to 1686 B.C.: "Hammurabi,
the shepherd, called by Enlil, am I; the one who makes
affluence and plenty abound; who provides in abundance
all sorts of things for Nippur-Duranki . . . ."[17] This
self-predication, which continues for about eighty lines,
describes Hammurabi's accomplishments in areas such as
religion, politics, and law; in addition to Enlil, it
also mentions several other gods, such as Marduk and
Shamash, whom Hammurabi recognized and served.

A number of inscriptions from Moab, Cilicia,
Syria, and Assyria, dating from the ninth or eighth

century B.C., illustrate the continuation of this "I am"
style of speaking.[18] It is typical of these inscriptions
that a king identifies himself with the words "I am,"
gives his titles, cites the name of a divinity from whom
he receives authority, and describes his accomplishments
as king. In these respects the inscriptions are similar
to the earlier self-predications from Sargon I and
Hammurabi. They suggest that a rather loose pattern of
self-predication existed in the ancient Near East, by
which a king announced his name and placed his claims
before his subjects. Although the pattern was evidently
not rigid in structure, the kings undoubtedly used it as
a way of enhancing the status and authority that they
claimed for themselves.

For our present study the most interesting
example of royal self-predication occurs in the Cyrus
Cylinder, in which Cyrus of Persia gives his own account
of his entry into Babylon: "I am Cyrus, king of the
world, great king, legitimate king, king of Babylon,
king of Sumer and Akkad . . . whose rule Bel and Nebo
love, whom they want as king to please their hearts."[19]
This self-predication appears near the middle of the
inscription, where the style changes from third-person
narrative to first-person account. Following the self-
predication, Cyrus describes the program of social
reform that he instituted in Babylon with the approval
of the city's own god, Marduk. II Isaiah, who hailed
Cyrus as the "one from the east" (Is. 41:2), would
undoubtedly have agreed with the implicit claim of the
Cyrus Cylinder that Cyrus was an enlightened, humane
ruler. II Isaiah clearly believed, however, that
Yahweh, rather than any other god, was guiding the
successful career of Cyrus. For this reason it may not
be accidental that II Isaiah so frequently uses the

self-predication "I am Yahweh" in passages that refer
to Cyrus (Is. 41:1-4; 43:8-13, 14-21; 44:24-28; 45:1-13).
Whether or not II Isaiah was directly acquainted with
the Cyrus Cylinder, he undoubtedly believed that a true
interpretation of the career of Cyrus would have to
begin with the words "I am Yahweh" rather than "I am
Cyrus."

       Several other passages in the Old Testament
suggest that human self-predications in the "I am"
style can actually represent claims to the status and
honor that belong to God alone.   In the seventh century
B.C., the prophet Zephaniah anticipated the destruction
of Nineveh because it made the pretentious claim, "I am
and there is none else" (Zeph. 2:15).   In the sixth
century B.C., Ezekiel predicted the downfall of the
prince of Tyre because he asserted, "I am a god" (Ezek.
28:2, 9).   In a similar way II Isaiah announced the
destruction of Babylon because of its arrogant claim,
"I am, and there is no one besides me" (Is. 47:8, 10).
II Isaiah makes it especially clear that Babylon's
claim is a parody of Yahweh's own self-predication,
"I am God, and there is no other" (Is. 45:22; 46:9).
As these references suggest, Zephaniah, Ezekiel, and
II Isaiah were evidently aware of the "I am" style of
speaking in surrounding countries.   They also perceived
how readily human self-predication could become a claim
to divinity, as people, cities, or countries attributed
to themselves the unique status or authority that
belonged to God alone.

       Our purpose in this section of our study has
been to look at examples of self-predication in the
ancient Near East as illustrations of an "I am"
rhetorical style with which II Isaiah and his audience
may have been acquainted.   We have seen that divine

self-predications are rather frequent, especially in
oracular forms that bear some resemblance to the
salvation oracle in II Isaiah. We have also seen that
an "I am" style of human self-predication occurs from
very early times in the ancient Near East, often in a
loose pattern in which a king states his identity and
makes known his claims. We have seen too that some Old
Testament writers, including II Isaiah, refer to a
"mixed" form of self-predication in which a human
speaker uses the "I am" style to make divine claims for
himself. Although we can not know exactly which examples
of the "I am" style II Isaiah was familiar with, it
seems clear in a general sense that he was acquainted
with both divine and human self-predications as these
formed a background for his own use of "I am Yahweh,"
"I am God," and "I am He."

CHAPTER III
Divine Self-Predication In Old Testament Sources

We may turn now to the next major part of our
study, in which we examine the use of divine self-
predication in Old Testament writings apart from II
Isaiah. Through this kind of analysis we will be in a
better position to understand any similarities or
differences between II Isaiah and other writers in
their use of self-predications. Most of the Old
Testament examples of divine self-predication occur in
writings or sources that were earlier than II Isaiah
himself. In this general sense they constitute the
background for II Isaiah's use of self-predications,
although it is not always clear whether he was directly
acquainted with specific writings or sources.

A. "I am Yahweh"

We may begin with the most common form of self-
predication, "I am Yahweh," postponing "I am God" and
"I am He" for later analysis. Apart from II Isaiah,
the statement "I am Yahweh" occurs 160 times in the Old
Testament.[20] Almost always "I am Yahweh" is simply ani
Yahweh, which occurs 150 times.[21] A longer form, "I am
Yahweh God," ani adonai Yahweh, occurs five times in
Ezekiel but nowhere else.[22] A variation for "I am
Yahweh," anoki Yahweh, occurs five times in several
different sources.[23] There is some evidence that anoki
Yahweh may represent a "northern" tradition of divine
self-predication, since it occurs in some sources that
may be of northern provenance (Ex. 20:2, possibly E;
the parallel in Deut. 5:6; two occurrences also in
Hosea). It has the same meaning, however, as ani

Yahweh. Similarly, Ezekiel uses ani adonai Yahweh in a
way that can not be distinguished from his use of ani
Yahweh. For these reasons we may treat all three
expressions together as forms of "I am Yahweh."

1. Early Narrative Sources

If we analyze the expression "I am Yahweh" in
terms of the sources in which it appears, we notice
first that it occurs a number of times in early narrative
traditions (J and E) dealing with events connected with
the Exodus from Egypt and the covenant at Sinai.[24] The
statement evidently did not occur in earlier periods of
the people's history.[25] It seems to occur first in the
time of Moses, in passages in which Yahweh is giving
instructions concerning the plagues in Egypt (Ex. 7:17;
8:22; 10:2), the Exodus from Egypt (Ex. 14:4, 18), and
the Sinai covenant (Ex. 20:2). The fact that Yahweh is
addressing Moses in most of these passages suggests
that the original setting for the divine self-predication
"I am Yahweh" was God's revelation of himself to Moses.
The early narrative sources also indicate, at the same
time, that God was seeking to reveal himself more
widely: the purpose of the plagues was to convince the
Pharaoh (Ex. 7:17; 8:22) or the people of Israel (Ex.
10:2) that "I am Yahweh," and one consequence of the
Exodus from Egypt was that "the Egyptians shall know
that I am Yahweh" (Ex. 14:4, 18). Yahweh's revelation
to Moses, as important as it was in itself, was closely
correlated with his working through historical events
to make himself known, in ever widening circles, to
his own people and also to others.

The early narrative sources (J and E) suggest
clearly that the statement "I am Yahweh" was a very

early form of divine self-predication that went back to the time of Moses. From a historical point of view, there would seem to be no reason to doubt that this was the case; indeed, as we shall see, later sources also confirm that "I am Yahweh" had its original setting in the time of Moses. In a theological sense, it is important to notice that the self-predication, from the very beginning, was associated with the themes of grace and law together. It introduced Yahweh as the God who freely took the initiative to deliver his people from bondage, and it also presented him as the God who asked his people to live according to his laws within the covenant relationship that he established. The self-predication in the covenant at Sinai illustrates this close connection between the themes of grace and law: "I am Yahweh your God, who brought you out of the land of Egypt, out of the house of bondage. You shall have no other gods before me . . . " (Ex. 20:2 ff.).

2. Hosea

The prophet Hosea provides relatively early confirmation of these historical and theological aspects of "I am Yahweh." Although he uses the expression only twice, he establishes a connection in both instances with the time of Moses, and he also shows the close correlation between the themes of grace and law. These aspects of the self-predication are especially clear in Hos. 13:4:

> I am Yahweh your God
>   from the land of Egypt;
> you know no God but me,
>   and besides me there is no savior.
>   (Hos. 13:4; cf. 12:9)

Hosea implies very strongly here that Yahweh's role as
the God of the people of Israel had its decisive
beginning with their experiences in Egypt, especially
in the Exodus deliverance from Egypt at the time of
Moses. Although Yahweh existed previously, and the
people themselves had an inchoate corporate existence
in earlier times, he first became their God "from the
land of Egypt." The grace that Yahweh showed by
delivering the people from bondage established a
covenant relationship in which they were expected to
follow his commandments. The first and most important
commandment, underlying all the others, was that the
people should acknowledge Yahweh alone as their God and
give their covenant loyalty to him alone.

       In these ways Hosea confirms the impression that
we receive from the early narrative traditions that
"I am Yahweh" had its original setting in the time of
Moses and that it embraced the themes of both grace and
law. Indeed, Hosea's use of this expression in Hos.
13:4 is a poetic counterpart to the prose statement,
which may come from the E document, at the beginning of
the Ten Commandments: "I am Yahweh your God from the
land of Egypt" is parallel to "I am Yahweh your God,
who brought you out of the land of Egypt . . . " and
"you know no God but me . . . " is parallel to "you
shall have no other gods before me." Hosea and the
author of the E document may have been contemporaries,
in the middle of the eighth century B.C.; both were
evidently from the northern kingdom; stylistically,
they concur in the rare use of the longer word for "I"
(anoki) in "I am Yahweh"; both add the appositive "your
God" in their use of the self-predication. If we may
assign the Ten Commandments to the E document, then it
is clear that Hosea and the author of E had much the

same sources of information for their understanding of
the historical and theological aspects of the statement "I am Yahweh."

3. The P Document

Data from the P document give further support to
these views concerning the original setting and significance of "I am Yahweh." The author of P wishes to
emphasize that God first revealed the name Yahweh to
Moses: "And God said to Moses, 'I am Yahweh. I appeared
to Abraham, to Isaac, and to Jacob, as God Almighty, but
by my name Yahweh I did not make myself known to them'"
(Ex. 6:2-3). In this way P suggests that the divine
self-predication had its original setting not only in
the time of Moses but in a scene of revelation to Moses
himself. At the same time, God commissions Moses to
make his name known to the people of Israel: "Say
therefore to the people of Israel, 'I am Yahweh, and
I will bring you out from under the burdens of the
Egyptians . . . '" (Ex. 6:6). As we saw in the case of
the earlier narrative sources J and E, Yahweh wishes to
act through historical events to make himself known
more widely. His private revelation to Moses points
beyond itself to his activity in history on behalf of
his people.
        Yahweh commissions Moses further to tell the
people of Israel of the covenant relationship that he
will establish with them: "and I will take you for my
people, and I will be your God; and you shall know
that I am Yahweh your God, who has brought you out
from under the burdens of the Egyptians'" (Ex. 6:7).
At this point the P document, with its reference to
covenant relationship, alludes to the theme of covenant

obligation or "law" and combines it with the motif of
the Exodus deliverance or "grace." Like J, E, and
Hosea, the P document links the self-predication "I am
Yahweh" with the themes of both grace and law. Finally,
in this central passage, God instructs Moses to tell
the people about the eventual conquest of Canaan: "And
I will bring you into the land which I swore to give to
Abraham, to Isaac, and to Jacob; I will give it to you
for a possession. I am Yahweh" (Ex. 6:8). As the
passage began with "I am Yahweh" and a reference to the
patriarchs, it forms a chiasmus now by ending with an
allusion to the patriarchs and the self-predication "I
am Yahweh" (Ex. 6:2-3, 8).

From a literary point of view, the statement "I
am Yahweh" appears at major points in the structure of
the entire passage (Ex. 6:2-8). It appears first at
the beginning of the passage, where it has a double
function: to introduce the passage as a whole, and to
give the content of God's revelation to Moses (Ex. 6:2).
It occurs next in vs. 6, where again it has a double
function: to state the content of the revelation that
Moses is to communicate to the people of Israel, and to
establish the link between "Yahweh" and the forthcoming
Exodus deliverance from Egypt. The self-predication
occurs a third time in vs. 7, where it serves to conclude the statement of the covenant formula and to
present Yahweh once again as the God of the Exodus
deliverance. Finally, the statement appears at the
very end of the passage, where it confirms the promise
of the conquest of Canaan and also brings the entire
passage to a conclusion.

This analysis of the structure of the passage
helps us to identify more clearly the setting and themes
that the author of the P document associates with the

self-predication "I am Yahweh" -- the original revelation of the special divine name to Moses, the communication of this revelation to the people of Israel, the
activity of God in history on behalf of his people,
the covenant relationship between God and the people,
and the close correlation between the motifs of grace
and law. In all of these respects the P document is
clarifying and systematizing ideas that the earlier
sources (J, E, and Hosea) had suggested in connection
with the statement of divine self-predication. We
receive the impression that the writer of the P document
is concerned to preserve early tradition and to transmit
it accurately, even though he arranges the passage as a
whole according to his own conceptions of structure and
balance.

In this passage that is so important for the
author of the P document we should notice that "I am
Yahweh" has the same meaning as "I am Yahweh your God."
The shorter statement occurs three times, in Ex. 6:2,
6, and 8, and the longer form occurs once, in Ex. 6:7.
Since the appositive "your God" emphasizes the relationship between Yahweh and Israel, it is appropriate to
use "I am Yahweh your God" in connection with the
covenant formula, "I will take you for my people, and
I will be your God." Perhaps for the same reason the
E document and Hosea, as we saw above, use "I am Yahweh
your God" in contexts dealing with the covenant. The
J document, as far as can be determined, probably used
only the shorter form, "I am Yahweh."[26] The author of
the P document clearly uses both forms with the same
meaning, since he connects them both with the basic
theme of Yahweh's redemptive activity in history (Ex.
6:6-8). Even if some later Old Testament writers
attributed different emphases or different meanings to

these two forms of self-predication, the data from early sources indicate that originally, at least, the two forms had the same meaning.[27]

A number of other examples of "I am Yahweh" in the P document occur in passages that refer in some way to the Exodus from Egypt. These passages deal with the message that Moses is to give to Pharaoh (Ex. 6:29), the passover preceding the Exodus (Ex. 12:12), the Exodus deliverance itself (Ex. 7:5), and the provision for food following the escape into the wilderness (Ex. 16:12). Sometimes the statement "I am Yahweh" appears at the beginning of God's words, as a way of introducing and authenticating them (Ex. 6:29; cf. 6:2, 6); more typically, "I am Yahweh" appears at the close of a thought or a passage as a way of emphasizing the authority of the speaker (Ex. 12:12; 16:12; 29:46; 31:13; Num. 3:13, 45; 10:10; 15:41). Sometimes God undertakes a course of action so that "the Egyptians shall know that I am Yahweh" (Ex. 7:5); more often, however, he gives explanations or instructions to Moses, as representative of the people, so that "you shall know that I am Yahweh your God" (Ex. 16:12).

Throughout his work the author of the P document continues to use the formula "I am Yahweh" in passages that combine the themes of Exodus deliverance and covenant obligation. "For I am Yahweh who brought you up out of the land of Egypt, to be your God; you shall therefore be holy, for I am holy" (Lev. 11:45). When Yahweh speaks in this way to his people, he reminds them of his grace in taking the initiative to deliver them from Egypt, and he also reminds them of his expectation that they will live in an appropriate manner -- in holiness -- as his covenant people. The word "therefore" is especially significant here because

it illustrates the relationship between grace and law:
Yahweh has shown his grace to his people; therefore,
he asks them to live according to his law. From
another point of view, this relationship means that the
people accept covenant obligation as a way of respond-
ing in gratitude to the grace that Yahweh has already
shown. The author of P reflects this point of view
when he speaks of law and then grace: "So you shall
remember and do all my commandments, and be holy to
your God. I am Yahweh your God, who brought you out of
the land of Egypt, to be your God: I am Yahweh your God"
(Num. 15:40-41). The fact that the writer uses the
shorter formula "I am Yahweh" in Lev. 11:45 and the
longer formula "I am Yahweh your God" in Num. 15:41
confirms, as we have already seen on the basis of Ex. 6,
that he uses them with the same meaning -- i.e., both
forms of self-predication are connected with both
themes, grace and law.

Although most of the P document does consist of
instructions and regulations that God gives Moses to
deliver to the people of Israel, the writer is clearly
aware that God's grace precedes his law and forms the
theological basis for the expectations that he places
upon his people. In this respect the author of P
perceives the same relationship between grace and law
as the author of E and the prophet Hosea. Our analysis
has shown that all three use the self-predication "I am
Yahweh" in contexts that combine the themes of grace
and law in such a way that the former precedes and
underlies the latter. When we analyze II Isaiah's use
of the divine self-predication, we will ask whether he
too associated it with both grace and law. II Isaiah,
as we shall see, clearly connected the formula "I am
Yahweh" with the imminent redemption of the exiles in

Babylon; in the light of earlier Old Testament usage,
we will ask whether he also associated the phrase with
the theme of covenant obligation.

To conclude our analysis of "I am Yahweh" in the
P document, we may look at a passage in which Yahweh's
self-predication is brought into connection with his
presence at the tent of meeting. After giving
instructions concerning the morning and evening offer-
ings before the tent of meeting, God comments on the
tent of meeting itself:

> It shall be a continual burnt offering
> throughout your generations at the door
> of the tent of meeting before the Lord,
> where I will meet with you, to speak
> there to you. There I will meet with
> the people of Israel, and it shall be
> sanctified by my glory; I will consecrate
> the tent of meeting and the altar; Aaron
> also and his sons I will consecrate, to
> serve me as priests. (Ex. 29:42-44)

The passage continues with a modified version of the
covenant formula that emphasizes God's "dwelling" among
his people: "And I will dwell among the people of
Israel, and will be their God" (Ex. 29:45; cf. 6:7).
The concluding verse, carefully arranged and balanced,
begins with a divine self-predication, refers to the
Exodus from Egypt, speaks again of God's "dwelling"
among his people, and ends with another self-predication:
"And they shall know that I am Yahweh their God, who
brought them forth out of the land of Egypt that I
might dwell among them; I am Yahweh their God" (Ex. 29:
46; cf. 6:7).

This passage is especially important because it
is the only point at which the P document specifically

associates the formula "I am Yahweh" with the tent of
meeting. The passage itself may well belong to a later
stratum of the P document or represent a relatively
late addition, since the awkward transition in vs. 42
from the third person "Lord" to the first person "I"
points to the composite nature of the text. The fact
that in the same verse the word "you" is at first plural
and then singular also suggests that the passage has
been fitted with some difficulty into its present
setting. The writer clearly wished, however, to
emphasize the theme of God's gracious dwelling with his
people, and he wished to correlate this theme with the
theological perspective that he found already present
in the P materials themselves. In this respect the
passage does have a legitimate place as part of the P
document.

To appreciate the significance of this passage
in Ex. 29:42-46, we may recall first that earlier
tradition had regarded the tent of meeting as an
oracular shrine set up outside the camp. On occasion
the "pillar of cloud" would descend to the door of the
tent, and Yahweh would speak there with Moses (Ex. 33:
7-11, probably E). Although there is some indication
that anyone could meet with Yahweh at the tent of
meeting (Ex. 33:7), this early view presents the tent
primarily as a place where Yahweh was occasionally
present to speak with Moses.

The P document continues to use the term "tent"
of meeting" and to depict the tent as a place where
Yahweh meets with Moses (Ex. 30:36). At the same time,
it uses other terms, such as tabernacle and sanctuary,
to express important aspects of the significance of the
tent. It also locates the tent in the center of the
camp to emphasize that it is God's holiness which

sanctifies the people. It views the tent as the focal
point of God's gracious presence among his people, and
it establishes a correlation between God's glory as it
appeared on Mount Sinai and his presence in the
tabernacle as Israel undertakes her desert journey.
In all these ways the P document significantly extends
the theological conception of the much simpler oracular
shrine that had appeared in earlier tradition.

To develop this conception of the tent of meeting, the P document first describes the "glory" of
Yahweh in terms of the "cloud" and "fire" on Mount
Sinai: "The glory of Yahweh settled on Mount Sinai, and
the cloud covered it six days . . . Now the appearance
of the glory of Yahweh was like a devouring fire on the
top of the mountain in the sight of the people of
Israel" (Ex. 24:16-17). One of the first commands that
God gives Moses on Mount Sinai is that the people should
construct the tabernacle: "And let them make me a
sanctuary, that I may dwell in their midst. According
to all that I show you concerning the pattern of the
tabernacle, and of all its furniture, so you shall make
it" (Ex. 25:8-9). By designating the tent as a
"tabernacle" (mishkan), the P document emphasizes that
God's purpose is to "dwell" (shaken) in the midst of
his people. By employing these related words, and
especially the technical term "dwell," the P document
seeks to modify the earlier view of the tent as a place
where Yahweh was only occasionally present. From the
very beginning of its own account, it speaks of the
tent as a "tabernacle" to indicate that God was
continually present with his people.[28]

Having described the glory of Yahweh on Mount
Sinai (Ex. 24:16 ff.) and his intention to have a
tabernacle that he may dwell among his people (Ex. 25:

8-9), the P document brings these two lines of thought
together in Ex. 40:34: "Then the cloud covered the tent
of meeting, and the glory of Yahweh filled the
tabernacle." The glory of Yahweh, which had settled
earlier on Mount Sinai, now fills the tabernacle so that
it can accompany the people when they set out on their
journeys: "For throughout all their journeys the cloud
of Yahweh was upon the tabernacle by day, and fire was
in it by night, in the sight of all the house of Israel"
(Ex. 40:38). God's presence on Mount Sinai, as awesome
as it was, did not mean that he was limited to that one
locality; through the tabernacle, he was still present
to his people and could accompany them on their
journeys.

On the basis of this understanding of the
tabernacle in the P document we can more fully
appreciate the intentions of the person who contributed
the passage in Ex. 29:42-46. In Ex. 25:8-9, this author
found the important thought that God wanted the
tabernacle so that he could dwell in the midst of his
people. In Ex. 6:2-8 the writer evidently found a
complex of ideas that included the self-predication of
Yahweh, the Exodus deliverance from Egypt, the covenant
formula ("I will take you for my people, and I will be
your God," vs. 7), and the eventual entry into the land
of Canaan. The author apparently drew ideas from these
two passages to construct his own statement in Ex. 29:
42-46. Here the idea of "dwelling" is prominent. It
appears now as part of the covenant formula itself
("I will dwell among the people of Israel, and will be
their God," vs. 45). It also appears as the purpose or
result of the Exodus deliverance ("who brought them
forth out of the land of Egypt that I might dwell among
them," vs. 46). In a similar way the self-predication

"I am Yahweh their God" is prominent in this passage.
It appears twice in the closing verse, evidently as a
way of assuring the people that the God who brought
them out of Egypt does indeed dwell among them.

The author of Ex. 29:42-46 expresses typical
priestly interests when he speaks of the tent of meeting, the altar, and the Aaronic priesthood (vs. 44).
In a general sense he also regards the tent of meeting
as the locus for Yahweh's "dwelling" among his people
and for his self-predication. It is significant,
however, that he subtly deemphasizes the connection
between these ideas and the tent of meeting. The idea
of God's dwelling with his people becomes part of the
covenant formula, so that it is most immediately
associated with the covenant reality itself rather than
with the tent of meeting as a cultic object. In a
similar way the self-predication "I am Yahweh their God"
is associated only in a general way with the setting
provided by the tent of meeting. It is connected most
directly with other realities that are determinative
for the author's faith -- the past event of the Exodus,
the covenant relationship between Yahweh and Israel,
and the continuing presence of Yahweh among the people
as part of the covenant relationship itself.

For these reasons we encounter the paradox that
Ex. 29:42-46 is the only passage in the P document which
associates "I am Yahweh" with the tent of meeting, yet
at the same time the author seeks to deemphasize this
connection as if it were not absolutely necessary. The
solution to this difficulty may lie in the author's
situation in the exilic or postexilic period. He
evidently knows of a liturgical practice from the days
when the Jerusalem temple was still standing, in which
the announcement "I am Yahweh," spoken by a priest or

a cultic prophet, was included in God's address to the
worshipers on some festal occasion. The divine self-
predication in Ps. 81:10 -- the only passage in the
Psalms in which the self-predication "I am Yahweh"
appears -- suggests that a liturgy of this kind had its
setting in the pre-exilic temple. The author of Ex.
29:42-46 looks forward to the resumption of such a
liturgical practice, and so he associates the announcement "I am Yahweh" with his account of the tent of
meeting in the Mosaic period. He is still living,
however, at a time when the temple has not yet been
rebuilt or its program of worship, at least, has not
been fully restored. For this reason he also wants to
indicate that the statement "I am Yahweh" can still be
meaningful apart from a liturgical setting in the
temple. He seeks to make this clear by deemphasizing
the connection between the self-predication and the
tent of meeting and by stressing the original connection
between the self-predication and the events of the
Exodus and the Sinai covenant. In this way, even at a
time when temple worship was still in abeyance, he can
assure his readers that Yahweh does indeed dwell among
them as the God of Exodus deliverance and covenant
relationship.

4. The Holiness Code

We may turn now to the Holiness Code of Lev. 17-
26, an independent complex of cultic and ethical
regulations that was apparently composed somewhat
earlier than the P document and then inserted into it
at a later time. As Eissfeldt has suggested, the
Holiness Code may have come into being as a distinct
collection not only during the exile but among the

exiles themselves in Babylon.[29] In this case the code
is especially important as an independent source for
the use of the formula "I am Yahweh." Apart from the
Holiness Code, the P document uses the divine self-
predication nineteen times; the Holiness Code itself
uses it 47 times.

The familiar injunction to love one's neighbor
provides a typical example of the way the Holiness Code
employs the divine self-predication to conclude and
reinforce a commandment: "You shall not take vengeance
or bear any grudge against the sons of your own people,
but you shall love your neighbor as yourself: I am
Yahweh" (Lev. 19:18). Here Yahweh is speaking to Moses,
explaining what he in turn should say to the people of
Israel (cf. Lev. 19:1-2). This setting is characteristic
of most of the examples of "I am Yahweh" in the Holiness
Code. Occasionally Moses receives instructions for the
priests (Lev. 21:1; 22:1) or for the priests and the
people together (Lev. 17:1; 22:17), but usually he is
told to address the people as a whole (Lev. 18:2; 19:1,
etc.). In structure, the injunction to love one's
neighbor consists of a commandment followed by "I am
Yahweh." The self-predication appears at the end as a
way of emphasizing the divine source of the commandment
and the divine authority that accompanies it; it reminds
the people that Yahweh himself has given the commandment
and expects them to obey it. With the exception of Lev.
18:2, where it introduces a series of commands, the
phrase "I am Yahweh" in the Holiness Code has this
function of concluding and reinforcing divine
commandments.

Although the injunction to love one's neighbor
illustrates the typical use of divine self-predication
in the Holiness Code, it is important to notice that

"I am Yahweh" also appears a number of times in passages that combine the themes of Exodus deliverance and covenant obligation. In a passage near the beginning of the code, for example, the self-predication appears in connection with each theme: "You shall do no wrong in judgment, in measures of length or weight or quantity . . . I am Yahweh your God, who brought you out of the land of Egypt. And you shall observe all my statutes and all my ordinances, and do them: I am Yahweh" (Lev. 19:35-37; cf. 22:31-33; 23:42-43; 25:38, 55; 26:12-13). In this particular passage the first self-predication appears in immediate conjunction with the reference to the Exodus, which in turn provides the basis for the injunction to "do no wrong in judgment"; the second self-predication is linked directly with a summary of covenant obligation. A number of other passages also connect "I am Yahweh" with the motifs of Exodus deliverance and covenant obligation. These passages are especially significant because they indicate that the Holiness Code does not simply use divine self-predication in a mechanical way to conclude and reinforce divine commands. Like the other sources that we have examined -- the early narrative sources, Hosea, and the P document -- the Holiness Code perceives "I am Yahweh" as the self-predication of the God who graciously delivered his people from bondage and then asks them to fulfill their responsibilities of covenant relationship. Like the other sources also, the Holiness Code presents the people's acceptance of covenant obligation as their response to the grace that Yahweh has freely shown in the Exodus deliverance.

In addition to connecting divine self-predication with the themes of Exodus and covenant, the Holiness Code, like the P document in Ex. 6:6-7, occasionally

brings out the close association between "I am Yahweh"
and the covenant formula. This is especially clear
toward the end of the code: if the people obey his
commandments, then, Yahweh promises, "I will walk among
you, and will be your God, and you shall be my people.
I am Yahweh your God, who brought you forth out of the
land of Egypt . . ." (Lev. 26:12-13). Echoes of the
covenant formula are also heard in Lev. 22:33; 25:28;
26:45. The fact that all of these passages connect "I
am Yahweh" with the Exodus deliverance as well as the
covenant formula indicates once again that the Holiness
Code, like the other sources that we have examined,
regards God's grace in delivering his people from
bondage as the basis of covenant relationship and
covenant responsibility.

       Although the Holiness Code undoubtedly contains
some very early materials, it evidently reached its
present form during the exilic period. The final chapter
in particular reflects the perspective of this time,
when the Jewish people in exile longed for some
reassurance that God had not forgotten them. The
chapter begins with a description of "blessings" and
"curses" that are similar to those in Deuteronomy 28
and are reminiscent also of ancient political treaties:
if the people obey Yahweh's commandments, he will bless
them (Lev. 26:3-13), but if they do not obey his
commandments, he will punish them (Lev. 26:14 ff.).[30]
These "blessings" and "curses" themselves may be very
early. As the curses continue, however, they seem to
reflect the events and problems of the exilic period.
Among the "curses" God warns now that he will scatter
his people among the nations, their own land will lie
desolate, and they will pine away in exile (Lev. 26:33,
39). The editor of this part of the Holiness Code,

like Jeremiah and Ezekiel, was trying to understand the disastrous events of the exile as God's way of punishing the people for their repeated failures to accept their covenant responsibilities.

The editor of this closing section of the Holiness Code carries the thought a step further by asking now whether the Jewish people in exile have any hope of regaining God's favor if they confess their wrongdoing and make amends for it (Lev. 26:40 ff.). Before the exile, Jeremiah and Ezekiel had argued that the people could still avert disaster because God would take account of true repentance and would react accordingly; God's sovereignty included his freedom to change his intentions in response to a change on the part of his people (Jer. 18; Ezek. 18). In a similar way, even though the exile has already begun, the editor of Leviticus 26 reassures the exiles that God will not reject them completely if they repent and change:

> Yet for all that, when they are in the
> land of their enemies, I will not spurn
> them, neither will I abhor them so as
> to destroy them utterly and break my
> covenant with them; for I am Yahweh
> their God; but I will for their sake
> remember the covenant with their fore-
> fathers, whom I brought forth out of
> the land of Egypt in the sight of the
> nations, that I might be their God:
> I am Yahweh.   (Lev. 26:44-45)

In this way the writer seeks to provide some meaningful basis of hope for the exiles, among whom he was very probably included. He warns the exiles that they must complete their punishment, and he very carefully refrains from mentioning any return to their

homeland (Lev. 26:43). Possibly because he is writing
rather early in the exilic period, he does not want to
raise expectations that might only lead to further
disappointment. Yet his faith finds its focus in
Yahweh's self-predication, which he gives twice in this
passage (Lev. 26:44-45) as a way of emphasizing its
importance to his readers. On the basis of this faith
he can reassure his readers that the God who graciously
brought their forefathers out of Egypt will continue to
be their God and will maintain his covenant relationship
with them.

In our analysis of the P document we saw that
the author of Ex. 29:42-46 associated the formula "I am
Yahweh" with the tent of meeting, yet at the same time
he deemphasized this connection to suggest that it was
not absolutely necessary. In this way he evidently
wished to indicate that the divine self-predication,
which had formerly played a role in the liturgical
practice of the Jerusalem temple, could still function
meaningfully during the exilic period to remind the
people that Yahweh continued to dwell among them as the
God of Exodus deliverance and covenant obligation.
Although the writer apparently looked forward to the
eventual resumption of the temple liturgy, he wanted to
emphasize that the divine self-predication could still
be a means by which God addressed his people apart from
a liturgical setting.

It may be significant in this respect that the
Holiness Code establishes only a very loose connection
between the sanctuary and the divine self-predication:
"You shall keep my sabbaths and reverence my sanctuary:
I am Yahweh" (Lev. 19:30; cf. 21:12, 23; 26:2). Here
the writer uses the self-predication to conclude and
reinforce a commandment concerning the sanctuary, but

he does not indicate that the self-predication itself
had a liturgical setting in the sanctuary. Since the
term "sanctuary" (miqdash) can refer to the tabernacle
of the wilderness period (e.g., Ex. 25:8) or to the
temple in Jerusalem (e.g., Ex. 15:17), the writer
apparently wishes to stress the essential independence
of "I am Yahweh" from the liturgical practice of the
temple. Like the author of Ex. 29:42-46, the author of
the Holiness Code finds it more meaningful, during the
period of the exile, to emphasize that the divine self-
predication still retains its original association with
the themes of Exodus deliverance and covenant obligation.
In this way, even though the temple lies in ruins, he
affirms that God can still address his people, reassure
them in their present situation, and give them a basis
of hope for the future.

In our analysis of the P document we also saw
that it uses the expressions "I am Yahweh" and "I am
Yahweh your God" with the same meaning. In a similar
way we may notice that the Holiness Code, at least in
its present form, uses both forms of self-predication
in essentially the same way. In connection with the
theme of Exodus deliverance or some other gracious act
on the part of Yahweh, it uses the shorter formula twice
and the longer formula seven times.[31] In connection
with the people's obligation to obey Yahweh's commandments, the Holiness Code uses the shorter formula 24
times and the longer formula 14 times.[32] The fact that
the shorter formula is used more often to express the
theme of "law," and the longer formula is used more often
to express the theme of "grace," could suggest that
there is some difference in emphasis between the two.[33]
It is important to recognize, on the other hand, that
both formulas appear in conjunction with both themes,

law and grace. In a number of instances the two
formulas have the same meaning within the same passage
(Lev. 18:2-5; 26:1-2, 44-45). These data all together
indicate that in the present form of the Holiness Code
the two forms of self-predication have essentially the
same meaning, even if "I am Yahweh your God" sometimes
emphasizes God's gracious activity on behalf of his
people and "I am Yahweh" sometimes underlines his
expectation that the people will fulfill their covenant
obligations.

5. Ezekiel

The prophet Ezekiel, to whom we may now turn,
was active during the early years of the sixth century
B.C., perhaps about the same time that the Holiness Code
was compiled and some years before the writing of the
P document. These three sources together account for
the great majority of the examples of "I am Yahweh" in
the Old Testament. Apart from II Isaiah, the expression
occurs 160 times. The Holiness Code uses it 47 times,
the P document 19 times, and Ezekiel 66 times, for a
total of 132 occurrences out of the 160. It is significant that these three sources all date from the sixth
century and are all trying to interpret the meaning of
the fall of Jerusalem and the exile in Babylon. It is
very possible, too, that all three sources were written
or compiled by Jewish exiles in Babylon rather than the
people who remained at home in Judah. It may also be
significant that these sources all reflect priestly
interests and points of view, although Ezekiel, more
directly than the others, combines these with a vivid
prophetic critique of the events of the day. As we
continue with our study, we shall look for some way of

explaining the fact that the formula "I am Yahweh"
occurs predominantly in sources that date from the
sixth century B.C., derive very possibly from the exile
itself, and reflect priestly interests.

Ezekiel almost always uses the short form of
self-predication, "I am Yahweh." He uses the longer
form, "I am Yahweh your (their) God," only seven times
(Ezek. 20:5, 7, 19, 20; 28:26; 39:22, 28). Elliger
has suggested that a more frequent use of the longer
form would have detracted from Ezekiel's emphasis on
the honor and holiness of Yahweh.[34] In Ezekiel's usage,
however, the longer form represents the themes of grace
(Ezek. 20:5; 28:26), law (Ezek. 20:7, 19, 20), or both
together (Ezek. 39:22, 28). In these respects it would
not appear to differ from the brief "I am Yahweh."
Ezekiel also uses a distinctive form of self-predication,
"I am Yahweh God," which occurs nowhere else (Ezek. 13:9;
23:49; 24:24; 28:24; 29:16). Although this self-
predication sounds especially formal and solemn, it is
used to reinforce several different ideas -- the
punishment of Israel (Ezek. 13:9; 23:49; 24:24), the
punishment of Egypt (Ezek. 29:16), and the restoration
of Israel (Ezek. 28:24). These are typical ideas that
Ezekiel also expresses with the simple formula, "I am
Yahweh." There is no reason to believe, therefore,
that "I am Yahweh God" differs in substance from the
shorter formula. Like "I am Yahweh your God," the
formula "I am Yahweh God" enriches the style of the
prophet's writing but is not associated with specific
themes that would differentiate it from "I am Yahweh."

A more important characteristic of Ezekiel's
writing is that an introductory statement, "you (they)
shall know that . . . " almost always precedes the
self-predication "I am Yahweh." When Ezekiel writes of

disasters that will befall the people of Judah, for
example, he represents Yahweh as saying, "According to
their way I will do to them, and according to their own
judgments I will judge them; and they shall know that
I am Yahweh" (Ezek. 7:27). Of the 66 times that Ezekiel
uses the formula of divine self-predication, he employs
this introductory statement in all instances except
three (Ezek. 20:5, 7, 19). This frequency of use, which
is especially characteristic of Ezekiel, suggests that
the introductory statement was an essential part of his
understanding of the significance of the self-predication
"I am Yahweh."

     It is clear that Ezekiel did not invent the
introductory statement, "you (they) shall know that. . ."
The statement occurs in early narrative sources which
deal with the time of Moses (Ex. 7:17; 8:22; 10:2;
14:4, 18), and these sources, in all probability, were
composed some centuries before the time of Ezekiel
himself. The statement is also present in the P document
(Ex. 6:7; 7:5; 16:12; 29:46; 31:13), although it is
completely absent from the Holiness Code (Lev. 17-26).
Ezekiel received this introductory statement from the
tradition available to him and evidently found it so
meaningful that he used it much more often than any
previous writer. His special contribution was to
perceive the close link that exists, or should exist,
between human "knowing" and divine self-predication.
This is evidently the reason why he almost always uses
the statement "you (they) shall know that . . ." before
the self-predication "I am Yahweh."

     Commenting on this link between the introductory
statement and the divine self-predication, Zimmerli has
observed that the revelation of Yahweh's name calls the
people of Israel to participate in a history that moves

through circumstances and events to a goal that can be
described only in terms of the initial revelation
itself: "I am Yahweh," in effect, stands at the beginning and at the end of Israel's history.[35] Yahweh
initiates the history of his people by revealing himself
to them, and then he continues to work through their
history so that they will know him more completely.
Throughout this history he acts, as Ezekiel often
indicates, for the sake of his "name." Because his name
represents his innermost identity, acting for the sake
of his name means that Yahweh acts on the basis of what
he is rather than what Israel is. Because the revelation of his name stands at the beginning and end of
Israel's history, acting for the sake of his name also
means that Yahweh acts in continuity with his initial
revelation and in consonance with the full understanding
of himself that he wants his people to have. More than
any other writer, Ezekiel has perceived and expressed
these aspects of the self-predication "I am Yahweh."

In his study of the statement "you (they) shall
know that . . . ," Zimmerli has argued that God's own
action, rather than human effort, establishes the
conditions for man's knowledge of God. First God acts
in a certain way in history, and then man receives a
fuller understanding of the meaning of God's self-
predication "I am Yahweh."[36] This knowledge is not an
abstract description of God's being but an occurrence
in response to God's action in history.[37] Because it
involves obedience to God's will, this "knowledge" is
also an "acknowledgement" of God.[38] In content, it
signifies that Yahweh acts faithfully toward Israel
through his intervention in her history, sometimes
revealing himself in judgment against her and sometimes
delivering and restoring her.[39]

Zimmerli believes that the original setting of
the self-predication "I am Yahweh" was a theophany in
which Yahweh introduced himself and made himself known
by revealing his innermost secret, his name.[40] Our own
study confirms this view, since we have seen that the
early narrative sources imply, and the P document
clearly indicates, that the self-predication "I am
Yahweh" was originally connected with God's revelation
to Moses. Zimmerli believes further that the introductory statement, "you (they) shall know that . . . ,"
did not originate in any specific setting, either prophetic or priestly, but occurred in any situation in
which events could serve as "signs" helping people to
make decisions, especially decisions between alternate
possibilities.[41] This introductory statement and the
divine self-predication may have been joined together
in the context of liturgical celebrations, in which
some authorized person, speaking in Yahweh's name and
employing the divine "I," described the great events
of divine revelation or proclaimed divine law.[42]

Since Zimmerli and Elliger have both emphasized
the importance of chapter 20 as a basic source for
Ezekiel's use of the phrase "I am Yahweh," we may begin
our own study by looking at several verses in this
chapter:

> On the day when I chose Israel, I swore
> to the seed of the house of Jacob, making
> myself known to them in the land of Egypt,
> I swore to them, saying, I am Yahweh your
> God. On that day I swore to them that
> I would bring them out of the land of
> Egypt into a land that I had searched out
> for them, a land flowing with milk and
> honey, the most glorious of all lands.

> And I said to them, Cast away the
> detestable things your eyes feast on,
> every one of you, and do not defile
> yourselves with the idols of Egypt;
> I am Yahweh your God.
>   (Ezek. 20:5-7)[43]

It is especially important to note here that the divine
self-predication has its setting in a theophany, when
Yahweh chose the people of Israel and made himself
known to them. As in Ex. 6:2, the self-predication
represents the first words that God speaks when he
makes himself known and discloses his name. It is also
significant that the self-predication is associated
here with the themes of both grace and law. When God
introduces himself as Yahweh, he promises to bring the
Israelites out of Egypt into a new land, and he also
commands them not to give their loyalty to other gods
or to worship idols. In all these respects Ezekiel
faithfully reflects the structure of earlier tradition,
since a number of other sources, as we have seen, also
associate the formula "I am Yahweh" with a theophany to
Moses or Israel that takes place in Egypt, embraces the
themes of grace and law, and initiates a relationship
in which God will deal with Israel throughout the course
of her history.

        As Ezekiel develops the thought of this chapter,
it becomes clear that he regards the occurrences of the
wilderness period as a typological model for events of
his own day. As the Israelites were disobedient to
Yahweh during the wilderness period, so the Israelites
of Ezekiel's time have worshiped idols "to this day"
(Ezek. 20:31). As Yahweh originally passed judgment on
the Israelites in the wilderness, so he will institute
a new judgment in the "wilderness," presumably the

desert areas between Babylon and Judah, to determine
which exiles will be allowed to return home (Ezek. 20:
33-38). As Yahweh originally acted for the sake of his
"name," refraining from destroying the wilderness
generation completely, so he will act on the same basis
when he brings the exiles home: "And you shall know
that I am Yahweh, when I deal with you for my name's
sake, not according to your evil ways, nor according to
your corrupt doings, O house of Israel" (Ezek. 20:44).

In developing this typology, Ezekiel uses the
divine self-predication itself as a way of reinforcing
the parallels between the wilderness period and his own
time. Yahweh addressed the Israelites with his self-
predication when he gave them statutes and ordinances
in the wilderness (Ezek. 20:12, 19, 20, 26). He will
address them in a similar way when he brings them out
of exile, judges them once again in the "wilderness,"
and restores them to their own land (Ezek. 20:38, 42,
44). On a literary level this use of the divine self-
predication highlights the similarities between the
two periods and gives a sense of unity to the structure
of thought in the chapter. On a theological level it
enables Ezekiel to remind his fellow exiles that
Yahweh is still a God of grace and law, as he was when
he first began to work in the history of Israel. As a
God of grace, Yahweh seeks to deliver his people; as a
God of law, he must enter into judgment against them.
His grace will prevail because he will act for the sake
of his "name," just as he originally acted toward the
wilderness generation.

At the beginning of chapter 20, when he was
describing the beginning of Yahweh's dealings with
Israel, Ezekiel used the divine self-predication first
in connection with the theme of grace, and then in

connection with the theme of law. First Yahweh swore
that he would bring Israel out of Egypt into a new land,
and then he gave commandments for Israel to follow
(Ezek. 20:5-7). When he examines Israel's situation in
his own day, however, Ezekiel reverses this sequence of
events. First he expects Yahweh to punish the people
for their disobedience of his commandments, and then he
believes that Yahweh will restore those in exile and
renew the covenant relationship with his people.
Through both types of experience, punishment and
renewal, the people will have the opportunity to "know"
the meaning of the formula, "I am Yahweh." In accord-
ance with this sequence we may look at some of the
other passages in which Ezekiel uses the formula of
divine self-predication.

  Between the years 597 and 587 B.C., when he
himself was probably in exile in Babylon, Ezekiel
frequently used the formula of divine self-predication
to reinforce and validate the pungent criticisms that
he made of his countrymen who remained in Judah. He
uses this formula, for example, when he reproaches the
people for their idolatry (Ezek. 6:7, 13-14; 14:8;
23:49), for their disobedience to Yahweh's statutes and
ordinances (Ezek. 11:12), and for the "abominations"
that they commit (Ezek. 7:4, 9; 33:29). In all these
instances he warns that Yahweh will punish them for
their wrongdoing: "I will punish you for your ways,
while your abominations are in your midst. Then you
will know that I am Yahweh" (Ezek. 7:4).

  In a similar vein, Ezekiel uses the formula of
divine self-predication when he reproaches the false
prophets who mislead the people by saying "'Peace' when
there is no peace" (Ezek. 13:9, 14, 21, 23; cf. 13:10).
He also uses the self-predication when he warns his

countrymen about the danger of invasion (Ezek. 7:27),
the destruction of Jerusalem (Ezek. 12:20; 15:7; 24:24),
and the threat of exile (Ezek. 6:10; 11:10; 12:15-16;
22:16). He even uses the formula of divine self-
predication when he warns that Yahweh will punish the
surrounding nations (Ezek. 25:5, 7, 11, 17; 26:6;
28:22-23; 29:6, 9, 16, 21; 30:8, 19, 25, 26; 32:15;
35:4, 9, 15).

In connection with these numerous examples in
which Ezekiel indicates that he expects divine punishment to fall on his own people and on other nations, it
is especially important to notice that he almost always
uses the introductory statement "you (they) shall know
that . . ." before the formula of self-predication.
When he warns his countrymen of the threat of exile,
for example, he represents Yahweh as saying, "And they
shall know that I am Yahweh, when I disperse them among
the nations and scatter them through the countries"
(Ezek. 12:15). The use of the introductory statement
makes it clear that Yahweh does not act arbitrarily
when he punishes, nor does he punish merely because the
people have disobeyed his commandments. He is, indeed,
grieved and offended at their wrongdoings, and he
regards these as the cause for the punishment. But he
also punishes his people with the intention that they
come to "know" the meaning of his self-predication,
"I am Yahweh." This self-predication stood at the
beginning of their history as a covenant people, before
the Exodus from Egypt; it governs the course of their
history, whenever Yahweh acts for the sake of his name;
the full knowledge of the meaning of the self-predication
stands as the goal toward which their history is moving.
In this respect Yahweh's punishment of his people,
however justified, is not an isolated act but part of

their history in which he is working to bring them to a
knowledge of himself. Because it has a purpose as well
as a cause, the punishment is incorporated into the
broader context of the people's relationship with Yahweh
throughout their history.

In a number of instances, especially after the
destruction of Jerusalem in 587 B.C., Ezekiel also uses
the formula of divine self-predication to support his
promises of restoration and renewal. He uses this
formula, for example, when he reassures the exiles that
Yahweh will bring them back to their homeland. Yahweh
will do this, not because the exiles deserve it, but
because he will fulfill his promise to their fathers
(Ezek. 20:42) and he will act for his name's sake
(Ezek. 20:44; 36:23). The people will still have the
remembrance of their wrongdoings (Ezek. 20:42). But
they will have a new life and a new Spirit (Ezek. 37:6,
13; 39:28), and they will dwell in security and
prosperity (Ezek. 34:27; 36:11, 38). The neighboring
countries will no longer hurt them (Ezek. 28:24, 26),
and even countries far away will not threaten them
(Ezek. 38:23; 39:6, 7).

In a similar way Ezekiel uses the formula of
self-predication when he looks forward to the renewal
of the covenant relationship between Yahweh and Israel.
As the basis of the covenant, Yahweh will forgive his
people (Ezek. 16:62). The people will continue to
remember their wrongdoing (Ezek. 16:62), but they will
experience such forgiveness that they will be able to
forget their shame (Ezek. 39:28). The new covenant
will be everlasting (Ezek. 16:62; 37:28), and it will
find a visible symbol in the new temple that Ezekiel
envisages in Jerusalem (Ezek. 37:28). In the context
of his discussion of the new covenant, Ezekiel maintains

contact with early tradition by using the old covenant
formula: "My dwelling place shall be with them; and I
will be their God, and they shall be my people" (Ezek.
37:27).

It is significant, once again, that Ezekiel
consistently uses the introductory statement "you (they)
shall know that . . ." before the formula "I am Yahweh."
Just as he uses this statement in the passages that warn
of punishment, so he uses it in those that promise
restoration and renewal. The reassurance of redemption,
no less than reproaches and warnings, belongs to the
meaning of the divine self-predication as the people
will come to "know" it through their historical
experience. Through restoration to their homeland and
renewal of their covenant relationship, the people of
Israel will gain new insight into the meaning of the
words that God uses to address them: "I am Yahweh."
Because exile and restoration are both events from which
the people can learn about God, Ezekiel occasionally
refers to both together: "Then they shall know that I am
Yahweh their God because I sent them into exile among the
nations, and then gathered them into their own land"
(Ezek. 39:28).

6. Other Sources

Up to this point our study of the expression "I
am Yahweh" has been based primarily on sources that use
these words a number of times -- the early narrative
sources, the P document, the Holiness Code, and Ezekiel.
Apart from II Isaiah, these writings provide most of
the data for the use of "I am Yahweh" in the Old Testament. We also looked briefly at Hosea, even though he
uses the divine self-predication only two times, since

his usage is so similar to that of the E document. To
complete our study of "I am Yahweh," we may turn now to
the other Old Testament writings that employ this phrase.
These writings are important in their own way, although
they uses the self-predication only one to four times.
They include Deuteronomy, Judges, I Kings, Psalm 81,
Jeremiah, Isaiah (apart from II Isaiah), Joel, and
Zechariah.

The book of Deuteronomy uses the divine self-
predication in 5:6, at the beginning of its rendition
of the Ten Commandments: "I am Yahweh your God, who
brought you out of the land of Egypt, out of the house
of bondage." Like the parallel in Ex. 20:2, and like
the very similar verse in Hos. 13:4, this verse uses
the longer word, anoki, for "I." Since all of these
passages may very possibly reflect northern traditions
of covenant renewal, the use of the longer word for "I"
in the divine self-predication may be a northern idiom.
Deuteronomy also uses "I am Yahweh your God" in 29:6
(Hebrew 29:5), where the expression is associated with
the theme of God's gracious guidance in the wilderness.
God led his people for forty years in the wilderness, so
that they might know the meaning of his self-predication,
"I am Yahweh your God."

In the book of Judges the self-predication occurs
only once, in the speech of an anonymous prophet at the
time of the Midianite invasions. When the Israelites
cried for help because of the Midianites, the prophet
said to them, "Thus says Yahweh, the God of Israel: I
led you up from Egypt, and brought you out of the house
of bondage . . . and I said to you, 'I am Yahweh your
God; you shall not pay reverence to the gods of the
Amorites, in whose land you dwell.' But you have not
given heed to my voice" (Judg. 6:8-10). Although the

present form of the book of Judges may come from
Deuteronomic editors of the late seventh or early sixth
centuries B.C., several factors indicate that the
substance of this account, including the use of the
divine self-predication, may be very early: the account
belongs to the narrative material, rather than to the
framework in which the viewpoint of the editors is
especially evident; the words of an anonymous "prophet"
would not have been added at a later date to compete
with the story of Gideon, the major hero in the defense
against the Midianites; the self-predication itself,
which could easily be omitted here, must have been
included because it originally belonged to the substance
of the incident.

     If these arguments are correct, then this speech
of the anonymous prophet constitutes an important source
for the use of the formula "I am Yahweh" at a time rather
early in the period of the Judges. The close connection
with the Exodus from Egypt confirms the conclusion that
we have drawn on the basis of other sources, especially
the P document and Ezekiel, that the original setting of
the self-predication was a theophany to Moses (or Israel)
at the time of the Exodus. As in other sources, too,
the self-predication is associated here with the themes
of Exodus deliverance and covenant obligation -- i.e.,
grace and law. The theme of covenant obligation is
formulated here with special reference to conditions in
the land of Canaan. Instead of the general prohibition
not to have any gods besides Yahweh, as the first
commandment is stated in Exodus 20, covenant obligation
here assumes the form of not paying reverence to "the
gods of the Amorites." In these ways the speech of the
anonymous prophet preserves ideas with which the divine
self-predication was traditionally associated, and at

the same time it illustrates how the theme of covenant obligation could be restated with specific reference to Israel's new life in Canaan.

There is some possibility that the anonymous prophet was quoting from a service of covenant renewal when he cited the words, "I am Yahweh your God; you shall not pay reverence to the gods of the Amorites, in whose land you dwell." The formula of self-predication is not necessary in the structure of the prophet's speech; in fact, it interrupts the flow of thought as the speech proceeds from the recital of Yahweh's deeds on behalf of Israel to his demand that Israel not worship the gods of the Amorites. The prophet must have included the divine self-predication because his listeners were familiar with it in connection with the statement of covenant obligation. Although we can not be certain, it is possible that the prophet was quoting at this point from a ceremony of covenant renewal, early in the period of the Judges, in which the formula of divine self-predication was linked with a statement of covenant obligation in the specific form of a prohibition against worshiping the gods of the Amorites. In this connection it may be significant that the expression "the gods of the Amorites" occurs elsewhere only once, in Josh. 24:15, where it forms part of the ceremony of covenant renewal that the Israelites held at Shechem after their entry into Canaan. Like the prophet's speech in Judges 6, this passage also challenges the people not to worship "the gods of the Amorites in whose land you dwell."

The theory that the anonymous prophet in Judges 6 is quoting from a service of covenant renewal receives indirect support from the form of the speech itself. The messenger formula, "thus says Yahweh," introduces the speech and presents it as an authentic message that

the prophet brings from God. Within this speech the
formula of self-predication, "I am Yahweh," can have
only a secondary setting. It has no intrinsic
connection with the prophetic messenger speech but has
been incorporated into it from another context. The
prophet apparently used the formula of self-predication
at this point because he assumed that his listeners
were familiar with it from its setting in a service of
covenant renewal much like the one described in Joshua
24.

The first book of Kings contains two further
examples of the divine self-predication incorporated
into a prophetic messenger speech. In a number of ways
these two examples are very similar to each other. Both
occur in I Kings 20 (vss. 13 and 28) in connection with
the victories that Ahab of Israel won over Benhadad of
Syria. Both occur in passages spoken by an anonymous
prophet -- "a prophet" in vs. 13 and "a man of God" in
vs. 28. Both speeches begin with the messenger formula,
"thus says Yahweh." In content, both offer Yahweh's
promise of victory over the Syrians. Both indicate, as
a result, that "you shall know that I am Yahweh." The
second speech is especially significant because it
reflects a stage of thought, presumably contemporary
with the events of this chapter, at which other peoples
conceived of the Israelite God as solely a mountain God:
"Thus says Yahweh, 'Because the Syrians have said,
"Yahweh is a god of the hills but he is not a god of
the valleys," therefore I will give all this great
multitude into your hand, and you shall know that I am
Yahweh'" (I Kings 20:28).

Like the prophetic speech in Judges 6, these two
speeches in I Kings 20 illustrate how the formula "I am
Yahweh, originating as divine self-predication in

theophany, can be secondarily incorporated into a
prophetic messenger speech. In each case the position
of the formula indicates whether its relation to the
passage is intrinsic or secondary. The formula properly
stands at the beginning of a scene of theophany, for it
signifies how God introduces himself and gives his name
to the recipient of revelation (cf. Ex. 6:2). In a
prophetic speech, however, the formula of divine self-
predication may be incorporated wherever the structure
of thought requires. It may appear in the body of the
speech, as part of the argument (Judg. 6:10), or it may
appear at the end, as a way of indicating the result to
which the course of events will lead (I Kings 20:13, 28).

The two speeches in I Kings 20 are also significant because they combine the introductory statement
"you shall know that . . ." with the self-predication,
"I am Yahweh." Zimmerli, as we have seen, suggested
that this combination may have taken place in the
context of liturgical celebrations in which an official
person spoke in Yahweh's name.[44] Because these two
speeches in I Kings 20 contain no reflection of
liturgical practice, they can give no direct support to
Zimmerli's theory. We have seen, however, that the
expression "the gods of the Amorites" in Judg. 6:10
evidently had its original setting in a covenant renewal
ceremony much like the one described in Joshua 24. It
is possible that the introductory statement "you shall
know that . . ." was combined with the formula of self-
predication in the context of such a ceremony, and that
the combination then appeared without its liturgical
context in the prophetic speeches of I Kings 20.

Psalm 81, to which we may now turn, strengthens
the view that the formula "I am Yahweh," originating in
a theophany at the time of the Exodus from Egypt,

continued to function from a very early time in the
context of covenant liturgy. The opening verses, with
their references to singing, musical instruments, the
new moon, and "our feast day," indicate clearly that
the psalm reflects the ceremony of some festal occasion,
probably Passover or Tabernacles.[45] The central part of
the psalm gives the words of a cultic personage who
speaks on behalf of Yahweh, summarizing briefly the
Exodus from Egypt and related events, such as the
testing at Meribah and possibly the revelation at Mount
Sinai ("the secret place of thunder," vs. 7). In the
closing verses the speaker admonishes the people of
Israel for their disobedience and ingratitude, yet he
also expresses Yahweh's continuing wish to keep them as
his faithful covenant people.

     In summarizing the early history of Yahweh's
dealings with his people, the cultic speaker connects
the formula of self-predication with the themes of
Exodus deliverance and covenant obligation:

> There shall be no strange god among you;
>> you shall not bow down to a foreign god.
>
> I am Yahweh your God,
>> who brought you up out of the land
>> of Egypt.
>
> (Ps. 81:9-10)

When we compare these verses with similar passages,
such as Ex. 20:2-3 and Hos. 13:4, we notice that the
theme of covenant obligation has been placed in a
prominent position -- before the other elements rather
than after them. This proleptic placement emphasizes
the importance of covenant loyalty to Yahweh alone, and
it leads more naturally into the closing section of the
psalm, in which the speaker reproaches the people for
their lack of obedience to Yahweh. Theologically, it

remains true, as Ex. 20:2-3 and Hos. 13:4 indicate,
that covenant obedience represents the people's response
to Yahweh's revelation of himself and the grace that he
showed toward them in delivering them from Egypt.

Although the exact occasion on which this psalm
was used remains uncertain, it was an established
festival (vs. 4) in which a cultic personage, speaking
in Yahweh's name, challenged the people to recall
Yahweh's actions on their behalf at the time of the
Exodus and renew their commitment to their covenant
obligations. In this connection Bernhard W. Anderson
has called attention to the parallels between Psalm 81
and the liturgy of covenant renewal described in Joshua
24. He has also emphasized that the theological
assumption of the psalm is the conditional nature of
the Mosaic covenant -- the view that Yahweh can reject
his people if they are disobedient.[46] Both of these
characteristics make it possible to think in terms of
an early date for the composition of the psalm. In a
similar way Harvey H. Guthrie, Jr., has argued that the
elements of the psalm can be understood only in terms
of the faith and institutions of premonarchical times.
He points out, for instance, that the psalm contains no
references to the kingship of Yahweh, the cult of the
monarchy, the temple in Jerusalem, or the cosmic
mythology of the surrounding culture.[47] These observa-
tions make it very likely that the psalm originated at
an early period in connection with a festival of
covenant renewal in which the formula "I am Yahweh"
functioned to remind the people of the themes of Exodus
deliverance and covenant obligation.[48] Even in later
times, after the temple had been built and the
theologies concerning David and Zion had arisen, this
festival of covenant renewal could have continued as an
important part of Israel's religious life.

Psalm 81 gives the only example in the entire
Psalter of the formula of divine self-predication, "I am
Yahweh." This is understandable when we recall that the
psalms, in general, contain the people's words to God
(or about God) rather than God's address to his people.
At the same time we should also notice that Psalm 46
offers a close parallel to the formula "I am Yahweh":
"Be still, and know that I am God. I am exalted among
the nations, I am exalted in the earth!" (Ps. 46:10).
This use of "know" in connection with an "I am" form
of predication provides some support for Zimmerli's
suggestion that the introductory statement "you shall
know that . . ." was joined with "I am Yahweh" in the
context of cultic celebration. Indeed, some inter-
preters believe that the self-predication in Psalm 46
was originally "I am Yahweh" rather than "I am God,"
although the use of the name Yahweh at several other
places in the psalm (vss. 7, 8, 11) weakens the theory
that it would have been altered in the self-predication
itself.[49] The reference to the city of Jerusalem in
vs. 4 (cf. Ezek. 47:1-12) indicates that Psalm 46 is
later than Psalm 81. Although the exact date is not
certain, Psalm 46 is important for our present study
because it shows that divine self-predication continued
to play a role in Israel's worship even after the rise
of the monarchy and the building of the temple in
Jerusalem.

The prophet Jeremiah uses the formula "I am
Yahweh" only four times. Perhaps the most notable use
occurs in the vision concerning the "good figs" and the
"bad figs," i.e., the Israelites who were taken into
exile in the first deportation in 597 B.C. and those
who remained at home in Judah. The exiles were the
"good figs" because Yahweh promised to restore them to

their own land as the nucleus of a new covenant people: "I will give them a heart to know that I am Yahweh; and they shall be my people and I will be their God, for they shall return to me with their whole heart" (Jer. 24:7). The fact that the two baskets of figs in this vision are placed "before the temple of Yahweh" (Jer. 24:1) may well indicate that Jeremiah regarded the temple, and assumed that his audience would regard it, as the locus in which the formula "I am Yahweh" was employed in cultic liturgy and was specifically associated with the verb "know." In this respect Jeremiah's usage confirms the evidence of Psalm 81 concerning the liturgical setting of the divine self-predication. Like his contemporary Ezekiel, Jeremiah also uses the expression "I am Yahweh" in conjunction with the old covenant formula, "they shall be my people and I will be their God" (cf. Ezek. 37:27-28; also Jer. 31:33).[50]

In chapter 24 in Jeremiah the formula "I am Yahweh" emphasizes God's grace in restoring the exiles, giving them a new "heart," and renewing the covenant with them. The other three examples of the formula in Jeremiah put more emphasis on the theme of law, for they all warn that Yahweh will punish his people if they do not fulfill their covenant obligations. In one instance the formula "I am Yahweh" specifically introduces the announcement, so characteristic of Jeremiah, that Yahweh is giving the city of Jerusalem into the hands of the Babylonians (Jer. 32:27). The other examples of the formula are connected with more generalized statements concerning Yahweh's expectation of righteousness on the part of his people (Jer. 9:24; 17:10). These examples occur in passages that have the nature of proverbs or wisdom sayings. The occurrence

of "I am Yahweh" in such passages illustrates how the
formula of divine self-predication, originating in a
theophany, can be incorporated into a secondary context.
In a similar way, as we saw earlier in the case of
Judges 6 and I Kings 20, the divine self-predication
could be incorporated into a prophetic messenger speech.

The fact that Jeremiah uses the formula "I am
Yahweh" only four times stands in sharp contrast to the
usage of Ezekiel, the Holiness Code, and the P document,
which use the formula 66, 47, and 19 times, respectively.
In a very broad sense these four sources may be regarded
as contemporaneous with one another, although Jeremiah
was somewhat earlier than the others. Jeremiah probably
began his career in 626 B.C. and ended it sometime after
the fall of Jerusalem in 587 B.C. Ezekiel, from the
indications in his writings, was active from 593 to 571
B.C. The Holiness Code may have been compiled during
the same period in which Ezekiel was active, and the P
document was evidently written somewhat later, about
550 B.C. Why then would Jeremiah use "I am Yahweh" so
seldom, when the other three sources use the formula so
frequently and actually account for most of the
occurrences in the Old Testament?

In dealing with this question we must recall
that Ezekiel, the Holiness Code, and the P document
have three characteristics in common: they all come from
the sixth century B.C., they were all probably written
by Jewish exiles in Babylon, and they all reflect
priestly interests. We must also remember that the
worship services of the Jerusalem temple provided a
liturgical setting in which God's self-predication, "I
am Yahweh," could be preserved as a basic form of
address to his people, reminding them of his unpre-
cedented grace toward them and urging them to fulfill

their covenant obligations to him. These data provide
the basis on which we may compare Jeremiah's use of "I
am Yahweh" with that of the other sources.

It is significant in this regard that Jeremiah
was somewhat earlier than the other sources. He was
active primarily before the destruction of the temple
in 587 B.C., whereas the other sources come from periods
that fell largely or entirely after this date. Jeremiah,
that is, knew that the formula "I am Yahweh" was still
being preserved in the worship of the temple, and
perhaps for that reason he felt less need to incorporate
it into his own speaking and writing. Once this
liturgical setting had been lost, on the other hand,
Ezekiel, the Holiness Code, and the P document would all
reflect the need to provide other contexts, both oral
and literary, for preserving the formula and applying
it to the situation of the people. By incorporating the
formula in written documents, in particular, these
sources were preserving it for a happier time in the
future when the temple could be rebuilt and its services
of worship could be resumed.

When we compare Jeremiah with Ezekiel, the
Holiness Code, and the P document, it is also very
significant that Jeremiah was active in Jerusalem,
whereas these other sources probably represent the work
of Jewish exiles in Babylon itself.[51] Jeremiah lived
in the religious center of the nation, where he was
constantly reminded of its religious traditions and
beliefs. The exiles in Babylon, on the other hand,
felt an acute need to reassure themselves that Yahweh
could be present among them in a foreign land. When
Ezekiel and the compilers of the Holiness Code and the
P document made such frequent use of the formula "I am
Yahweh," they were not simply preserving it in written

form after the temple had been destroyed. They were
also reminding themselves, in an existential sense,
that Yahweh was indeed present among them in their land
of exile, continuing to offer them his grace and calling
them to be his faithful covenant people. It was
probably for this reason, more than any other, that
these sources employed the divine self-predication so
frequently.

Another characteristic that Ezekiel, the Holiness
Code, and the P document have in common is that they all
reflect priestly interests. With this background they
are especially interested, as we have seen, in the
history of the formula "I am Yahweh," its relation to
the themes of grace and law, and its preservation in a
cultic setting. Although Jeremiah himself was of a
priestly family, his responsibilities as a prophet
evidently eclipsed many of the interests that he might
have developed as a priest. He was especially critical,
for instance, of the false confidence that the people
placed in the temple as a guarantee of Yahweh's blessing
and protection, and he risked his life in trying to
correct this false belief concerning the meaning of the
temple (Jer. 7:26). Perhaps for this reason he was
reluctant to abstract the formula "I am Yahweh" from
its setting in temple worship and incorporate it
extensively into his own preaching. He may well have
felt that other phrases and expressions from religious
tradition were more suitable for communicating the
prophetic message that he was bringing to the people of
his time.

To complete our study of "I am Yahweh" in the
Old Testament we may look briefly at the few remaining
examples that we have not examined so far. It is very
likely that all of these examples come from post-exilic

writings, although it would go beyond the scope of the
present study to examine in detail the theories
concerning the date of these sources. A typical example
from this group is Is. 60:22, in which Yahweh is
promising that he will make his people prosper in their
own land:

> The least one shall become a clan,
>   and the smallest one a mighty nation;
> I am Yahweh;
>   in its time I will hasten it.
>
>   (Is. 60:22)

In a very similar way the other examples of "I am
Yahweh" in this section of Isaiah also occur in contexts
in which Yahweh assures his people that he will make
them prosper and will bless them in the sight of the
nations (Is. 60:16; 61:8). The late post-exilic example
in Is. 27:3 speaks of Israel as a vineyard to convey
the thought that Yahweh will protect her from her
enemies. An example from the book of Joel assures the
people, following a plague of locusts, that Yahweh will
restore prosperity to them (Joel 2:27). Another example
warns that Yahweh will judge the nations of the world,
but at the same time it also promises that Yahweh will
protect and support his own people (Joel 3:17; Hebrew
4:17). The fact that this self-predication has its
setting on Mount Zion in Jerusalem may indicate that
"I am Yahweh" by this time had been incorporated into
the liturgy of the second temple. The example of "I am
Yahweh" in Zech. 10:6 may be the latest of all, if
"Egypt" and "Assyria" (Zech. 10:10) refer to the
Ptolemaic and Seleucid dynasties. The example occurs
in a chapter dealing with the defeat of Israel's
oppressors and the restoration of the Jews to their
own land.

Because these examples of "I am Yahweh" are evidently all of post-exilic origin, they are important for the study of II Isaiah only in the sense that they illustrate the continuation of earlier contexts and themes. It is interesting, for instance, that all of these examples express the positive idea of Yahweh's blessing and protection for his own people. In this way the theme of God's grace, which was an essential aspect of the meaning of divine self-predication from the very beginning, found expression in a form suitable for the needs and conditions of the post-exilic period. Just as Yahweh originally relieved the oppression of his people in Egypt, so now, in the post-exilic period, he promises to relieve their oppression by foreign powers. During this period the formula "I am Yahweh" also has some connection with the theme of covenant responsibility, even though it is associated primarily with promises of grace and prosperity. Is. 60:21 expresses the expectation that "your people shall all be righteous" as they prosper once again in their homeland. Joel 2:27 links the divine self-predication with the principle that Yahweh alone is God; in this way it reminds the people of a basic tenet of their covenant relationship with Yahweh at the same time that it promises prosperity and blessing. Joel 3:17 promises that "Jerusalem shall be holy." The main thought here is that Jerusalem shall belong to Yahweh, so that "strangers shall never again pass through it." The writer may also be thinking that Jerusalem should be holy in an ethical sense, since he has previously warned of the need for repentance to avoid God's judgment on his own people (Joel 2:1-17).

From time to time we have seen some evidence for the view that the formula "I am Yahweh" had its original setting in a theophany at the time of Moses and then was

preserved in the context of liturgies of covenant
renewal, both before and after the construction of the
Jerusalem temple. We have also seen that Psalm 46
gives some support to the view that the introductory
statement "you shall know that . . ." was joined to the
formula of self-predication within a liturgical context.
Joel 3:17, which evidently reflects the cultic praxis
of the second temple, gives further support to both of
these theories. Since it presents Yahweh's words as he
appears and speaks in the temple, it also preserves the
original theophanic element in the divine self-
predication:

> And Yahweh roars from Zion,
>   and utters his voice form Jerusalem . . .
>   "So you shall know that I am Yahweh your God,
>   who dwell in Zion, my holy mountain."
>   (Joel 3:16-17)

B. "I am God"

We may turn now to a second major form of self-
predication, in which a word for "I" (ani, anoki) is
combined with a word for "God" (el, elohim). In
contrast to the word Yahweh, which is a proper name,
these words for "God" are rather general terms which
need to be made more specific if they are to be meaningful in a particular context. For this reason we find
that almost all the Old Testament examples of the
formula "I am God" have some additional word that seeks
to make the reference more specific -- e.g., "I am God
Almighty (ani el shaddai), Gen. 17:1; "I am the God of
your father" (anoki elohe abika), Ex. 3:6; "I am God,
your God (elohim eloheka anoki), Ps. 50:7. In the two
instances in which "I am God" stands by itself, the

context makes the meaning sufficiently clear. The
writer of Psalm 46 uses the name Yahweh several times
(vss. 7, 8, 11) to identify the speaker in vs. 10, "Be
still, and know that I am God" (anoki elohim). Hosea
uses the general word el to contrast the category of
"divinity" with "humanity": "I am God (el anoki) and
not man" (Hos. 11:9). At the same time, he also makes
the reference more specific by describing Yahweh as
"the Holy One in your midst," the one who "will not come
to destroy" (Hos. 11:9).

Because the words for "God" are rather general
in reference, it is not surprising that self-predications
of the type "I am God" occur very rarely -- only ten
times in the Old Testament, apart from II Isaiah.[52]
The expression occurs five times in Genesis as part of
the patriarchal narratives, in which God appears to
Abraham, Isaac, and Jacob to make promises or give
directions for a course of action (Gen. 17:1; 26:24;
31:13; 35:11; 46:3). The formula also occurs once in
Exodus, where it helps to link the patriarchal period
with the time of Moses: "I am the God of your father,
the God of Abraham, the God of Isaac, and the God of
Jacob" (Ex. 3:6). These first six occurrences all
suggest that the self-predication "I am God" had a
special association with the patriarchal period, at
least with regard to its original setting. In its
remaining occurrences the self-predication seems to
lack this particular reference to the patriarchal
period. Hosea uses "I am God (el)" to indicate the
status of divinity in contrast to humanity (Hos. 11:9),
and other writers use "I am God (elohim)" with obvious
reference to Yahweh (Pss. 46:10; 50:7; Ezek. 34:31).

In a number of instances the context of the
formula "I am God" indicates that the self-predication

occurred as part of a theophany to an individual person
(Gen. 17:1; 26:24; 31:13; 35:11; 46:3; Ex. 3:6). In
other instances the self-predication had its setting in
the worship of the temple (Pss. 46:10; 50:7). In these
respects "I am God" is parallel to "I am Yahweh," which
also originated in a theophany to an individual person
and then was preserved later in the context of temple
worship. The main difference is that "I am God"
evidently derived from the patriarchal period, whereas
"I am Yahweh," in all probability, originated in a
theophany to Moses.

In most of its occurrences, the self-predication
"I am God" is connected with the promise of some kind
of help or blessing that God will provide for the
recipient. To the patriarchs, for example, God promises
to give descendants (Gen. 26:24; 46:3) or both descendants and land (Gen. 17:1; 35:11). More generally, the
formula "I am God" introduces the promise of God's
continuing presence and blessing: "I am the God of
Abraham your father; fear not, for I am with you and
will bless you and multiply your descendants for my
servant Abraham's sake (Gen. 26:24; cf. Gen. 46:3; Ps.
46:10; Hos. 11:9; Ezek. 34:31). In several instances
the self-predication introduces God's promise to
undertake a specific action on behalf of the recipient,
such as bringing Jacob back from Egypt (Gen. 46:3),
delivering the Israelites from oppression in Egypt (Ex.
3:6), or releasing the Jewish exiles from their captivity
in Babylon (Ezek. 34:31). In most instances, therefore,
the formula "I am God" presents God as one who provides
for his people, blesses them, or delivers them from
oppression.

There is only one example in which the formula
"I am God" is directly connected with the theme of God's

judgment against Israel. Psalm 50 describes a theophany
in the temple, in which God "shines forth," summons his
covenant people to assemble, and assumes his role as
judge (vss. 2-6). Then he testifies against Israel:

> Hear, O my people, and I will speak,
>> O Israel, I will testify against you.
>> I am God, your God.

(Ps. 50:7)

At this point the formula "I am God" has evidently lost
its earlier association with the ideas of blessing and
deliverance, and it has been transposed into a different
setting, which may be regarded as the liturgical counterpart to the covenant lawsuit depicted by the prophets
(e.g., Hos. 4:1-3; Mic. 6:1-8). In this type of scene,
borrowed from the imagery of the law courts, God appears
as witness against his people and accuses them of failing
to fulfill their obligations under the terms of the Sinai
covenant. It is also part of the dramatic structure of
the lawsuit imagery that God assumes the role of judge
and indicates, directly or indirectly, the verdict of
"guilty" or the consequences that follow from Israel's
wrongdoing.

A comparison between the formulas "I am God" and
"I am Yahweh" reveals several similarities and also a
number of differences that will be important when we
analyze the usage of II Isaiah. Both formulas originated
in theophanies to individual persons, and in later times
both were utilized and preserved in the liturgy of the
Jerusalem temple. Both formulas could also express the
theme of grace, in the general sense that God would take
the initiative in some way to help his people.

The most striking difference between the two forms
of self-predication lies in their frequency of occurrence:
apart from II Isaiah, "I am God" occurs only ten times

in the Old Testament, but "I am Yahweh" occurs 160 times.
Undoubtedly the reason for this difference is that the
Hebrew words for "God" are rather general in reference,
especially against the background of polytheism in the
ancient Near East, whereas "Yahweh," as a proper name,
is much more appropriate for a self-predication. The
formula "I am God" goes back to the patriarchal period,
beginning with God's revelation to Abraham, but "I am
Yahweh" derives from God's revelation of himself to
Moses. In thematic content, "I am God" almost always
expresses the idea of grace -- specifically, God's
promises to provide for his people, the blessing of his
presence, or the benefits of his action. The occurrences
of "I am Yahweh," in contrast, usually reflect a particular writer's concern to maintain a creative tension
between the themes of grace and law, as these originally
found expression in the Exodus deliverance from Egypt
and the responsibilities that the people accepted under
the terms of the Sinai covenant.

C. "I am He"

So far, in our study of the Old Testament background to II Isaiah, we have examined the formulas "I
am Yahweh" and "I am God." We may turn now to the third
major type of self-predication, a succinct formula in
which God says simply "I am He" (ani hu). The statement
consists of the subject "I" (ani) and the predicate "He"
(hu); as in the other forms of self-predication, the
linking verb "am" is understood.

Although II Isaiah uses this type of self-
predication a number of times, it seems to occur
elsewhere in the Old Testament only in the Song of Moses
in Deuteronomy 32:

> See now that I, even I, am He (<u>ani</u> <u>ani</u> <u>hu</u>),
>   and there is no god beside me;
> I kill and I make alive;
>   I wound and I heal;
>   and there is none that can deliver
>   out of my hand.
>
>   (Deut. 32:39)

The introduction to the Song of Moses presents the poem
as a "witness" for Yahweh against the people of Israel,
because Yahweh anticipated that the people would worship
other gods and break their covenant with him after he
brought them into the new land of Canaan (Deut. 31:16-
22). The song presupposes that the people entered
Canaan some time ago, enjoyed a period of prosperity
there, and then became unfaithful to Yahweh by
worshiping other gods (Deut. 32:5-6, 15-21). Yahweh,
as a result, has determined to punish his people (Deut.
32:19-27), but he also promises that he will have mercy
on them afterward and will deliver them from their
enemies (Deut. 32:28-38). The Song of Moses as a whole
becomes an apologia on behalf of Yahweh, showing that
he is "just and right" in his dealings with his people
(Deut. 32:4).

In this context the poem represents Yahweh as
proclaiming, "I, even I, am He" (<u>ani</u> <u>ani</u> <u>hu</u>). The
self-predication depicts, first, the uniqueness of
Yahweh as the sole God; as the following words indicate,
"there is no god" beside him. Secondly, the formula
"I am He" conveys the sense of Yahweh's sovereignty
over the course of history. It brings to a climax the
poem's narration of events, in which Yahweh is at work
in the history of his people to choose them, lead them
into their homeland, punish them for their unfaithful-
ness, and eventually restore them once more. These two

aspects of the self-predication are closely related to each other. As the sole God in the world, Yahweh ultimately controls the course of history; conversely, his sovereignty over history demonstrates the uniqueness of his divine being.

In the structure of the poem the formula "I am He" also expresses the nature of Yahweh as the God who deals with his people in terms of both grace and law. Yahweh showed his grace by choosing the people of Israel, caring for them in the wilderness, and leading them into their homeland. As a God of law, he also expected that his people would fulfill their fundamental obligation under the covenant -- i.e., that they would worship him alone. In this respect "I am He" is parallel to "I am Yahweh," which also combines the themes of grace and law with special reference to Exodus deliverance and covenant obligation. "I am He," on the other hand, is less closely related to the formula "I am God," since this formula is almost always associated solely with the idea of God's grace.

Apart from II Isaiah, the self-predication "I am He" evidently occurs only in Deut. 32:39. The counterpart to this formula is the proclamation "I am," by which earthly powers or persons claim authority for themselves in a manner that amounts to an assertion of divine status. Nineveh, for example, boasts, "I am and there is none else" (Zeph. 2:15), and Babylon makes the claim, "I am, and there is no one besides me" (Is. 47: 8, 10). In these instances "I am" is simply "I" (ani); the Old Testament writers who formulated these claims may have felt that earthly powers, as proud and arrogant as they were, could not use the formula "I am He" (ani hu), which belonged to Yahweh alone. In the context of our present study the expression "I am" is important because it confirms that Yahweh's own self-predication, "I am He," involves the assertion that he alone is God.[53]

Old Testament usage also offers several parallels (in the second and third persons singular) which help to illumine the meaning of "I am He." When Jeremiah asks, "Art thou not He (halo attah hu), O Yahweh our God?" he clearly hopes for a response in the form "I am He" (Jer. 14:22). It is interesting that the context of this question refers to the uniqueness of Yahweh's divine being and his expectation that his people will fulfill their obligations under the covenant -- two aspects of the meaning of "I am He" that are prominent in the occurrence in Deut. 32:39. The affirmation in Psalm 102, "Thou art He (attah hu), and thy years have no end," refers to Yahweh's everlasting being as an aspect of his divine nature (Ps. 102:27; Hebrew 102:28). An example in the third person occurs in an address by Joshua to an assembly of the Israelites: "Yahweh your God is he (Yahweh elohekem hu) who fights for you" (Josh. 23:3, 10). Here "Yahweh" is subject and "he" is predicate; the sentence refers to the Israelite conquest of Canaan, understood here as an aspect of Yahweh's activity in history.[54]

The date of the Song of Moses in Deuteronomy 32 is uncertain. It evidently comes from a period long after the time of Moses, when Israelites must "remember the days of old" as they reflect on the beginnings of their existence as a people (Deut. 32:7). Eissfeldt dates the song in the eleventh century B.C., on the grounds that the summary of Israelite history ends with the conquest of Canaan and the subsequent apostasy, and the enemies mentioned in the poem suggest the Philistines.[55] G. Ernest Wright believes that the

imagery of harlotry as a metaphor for idolatry (Deut.
32:16) suggests a date later than Hosea, although he
also states, more generally, that the poem could have
been written any time between the periods of Elijah in
the ninth century and Ezekiel in the sixth. He also
makes the important observation that the lack of any
reference to exile in the poem argues against an exilic
or post-exilic date.[56] S. R. Driver assigns the poem
to a more limited period, the time of Jeremiah and
Ezekiel.[57]

Although the date of the Song of Moses is not
certain, we may notice certain parallels to the thought
and language of Hosea, Ezekiel, and Jeremiah that
suggest some general resemblance to their prophetic
spirit and perhaps also some proximity to their period
of activity. The Song of Moses, like the prophet Hosea,
divides the history of Israel into four periods. These
include God's original choice of Israel at the time of
Moses (Deut. 32:8-14; cf. Hos. 11:1, 3-4), Israel's
apostasy after entering Canaan (Deut. 32:15-18; cf.
Hos. 11:2), God's subsequent punishment of Israel (Deut.
32:19-27; cf. Hos. 11:5-7), and the eventual restoration
of Israel (Deut. 32:28-38; cf. Hos. 11:8-9). This
parallelism is the more remarkable because the Song of
Moses, like Hosea, speaks of the first two periods in
the past tense and regards the next two periods as still
to come. As metaphors for the restoration of Israel,
furthermore, both sources describe God's action with
the verbs "make alive" and "heal" (chayah and rapha;
Deut. 32:39, Hos. 6:1-2). The occurrence of these two
verbs together is rare elsewhere in the Old Testament.[58]

The Song of Moses also presents parallels to
Ezekiel and Jeremiah. The idea of Yahweh's "jealousy"
toward Israel's worship of other gods is echoed in

Ezekiel, although it also occurs elsewhere (Deut. 32:16,
21; cf. Ezek. 5:13; Ex. 20:5; Deut. 5:9). The explanation that Yahweh does not destroy Israel because other
nations would then consider him powerless, is parallel
to Ezekiel's principle that Yahweh will preserve Israel
as a way of vindicating the holiness of his name (Deut.
32:26-27; Ezek. 36:22-31). On a linguistic level, as
we have seen, the closest parallel to "I, even I, am He"
in Deut. 32:39 is Jeremiah's question, "Art thou not
He?" in Jer. 14:22.

Along with parallels such as these, a number of
differences between the Song of Moses and the other
sources indicate that the Song of Moses stands apart as
an independent document. The Song of Moses lacks
Hosea's clear reference to Assyria, Ezekiel's analysis
of Israel's sinfulness as beginning in Egypt itself,
and Jeremiah's specific mention of Babylon as the
instrument of Yahweh's punishment. Perhaps the poem
could best be assigned to a period later than Hosea but
before the exile of the sixth century B.C. For the
purposes of our present study, it would appear very
likely that the Song of Moses is earlier than II Isaiah.
Although we can not be sure whether II Isaiah was
directly acquainted with the Song of Moses, it provides,
along with Jer. 14:22 and Ps. 102:27, a source within
Israelite tradition from which he could have learned
of the expression "I am He."

CHAPTER IV
Divine Self-Predication In Second Isaiah

One of the most distinctive features of II
Isaiah's thought is his frequent use of statements
beginning with the words "I am," in which Yahweh makes
an assertion about himself that serves to define his
identity, describe his attributes, or depict his
relationship to Israel. Although these statements
assume several different forms, they may all be regarded
as self-predications in the sense that Yahweh is making
a significant assertion about himself that functions, at
the same time, to address his people at the most profound
level of their existence. In this regard the self-
predications stand in contrast to attributions beginning
with the words "Thou art," in which people make some
statement about Yahweh. The divine self-predications
also differ from human self-predications beginning with
"I am," in which persons or human organizations make
some claim for themselves. The divine self-predications
in II Isaiah are distinctive, not only because the
prophet uses them so frequently and in such a wide
variety of forms, but also because they stand in marked
contrast to these other forms of predication.

We can appreciate the significance of the
divine self-predications in II Isaiah when we notice
how the prophet treats them in relation to these other
forms of predication. II Isaiah frequently represents
Yahweh as saying, for example, "I am Yahweh," "I am
your God," or "I am He." These divine self-predications
constitute Yahweh's word to Israel, in which Yahweh takes
the initiative and reminds Israel of his own existence
and his relationship to her. We might expect that
Israel would respond to Yahweh's word with an attribution

beginning "Thou art," much as the author of Psalm 44,
in spite of the apparent hopelessness of exile, can
respond to God with the words, "Thou art my King and my
God" (Ps. 44:4). It is significant, however, that II
Isaiah records no response of this kind from his fellow
exiles in Babylon. He does urge them to respond to
Yahweh's word -- to sing "a new song" to Yahweh (Is. 42:
10) and "give glory" to Yahweh (Is. 42:12). He even
reminds the exiles that the Babylonians can address one
of their own idols with the attribution, "Thou art my
god" (Is. 44:17; cf. 42:17). But II Isaiah apparently
feels that Israel is still too discouraged to respond
to Yahweh's word, and he gives no passage in which the
exiles acknowledge Yahweh with the words, "Thou art my
God" or "Thou art He."[59] In this sense the divine self-
predications in II Isaiah are especially prominent
because they stand in contrast to a response that Israel
has not yet given. They become a poignant form of
address, in which a loving and caring God seeks to
elicit a response from his covenant people.

In a similar way II Isaiah contrasts Yahweh's
self-predications with the "I am" statements of Babylon
in chapter 47. Some of Yahweh's self-predications
express the uniqueness of his nature and being: "I am
the first and I am the last; besides me there is no god"
(Is. 44:6), "I am God, and there is no other" (Is. 45:
22; 46:9). In light of these assertions about Yahweh,
II Isaiah regards Babylon's own self-predication as a
claim to divinity as well as an assertion of uniqueness:
"I am, and there is no one besides me" (Is. 47:8, 10).
By formulating these predications in similar language,
II Isaiah wishes to indicate that both parties, Yahweh
and Babylon, are making assertions about themselves
that affect the very existence of Israel. Because

these claims are mutually exclusive, it follows that
Israel must choose between them. At the same time, II
Isaiah heightens the contrast between Yahweh and Babylon
by using slightly different wording in their respective
self-predications. Yahweh can say "I am God" or "I am
He" (ani hu; e.g., Is. 48:12), but Babylon can say only
"I am," which is literally the single word "I" (ani).
Even in the pretentiousness of her claims, Babylon can
not use the same language that Yahweh properly uses about
himself.

From a theological point of view, these contrasts
between Yahweh's self-predications and other types of
predication depict the situation in which Israel is
placed when she is addressed by Yahweh's word in a form
such as "I am Yahweh" or "I am your God." In this
situation Israel is summoned to respond to God with the
acknowledgment "Thou art my God," expressing in this
way her trust in God and her commitment to fulfilling
her role as the people of God. II Isaiah stresses the
importance of this response, even though he senses that
his fellow exiles are not yet ready to give it. When
Israel does finally make this response, she must be
careful to differentiate between "I am He" and "I am" --
i.e., between Yahweh's claims on her faith and loyalty,
and all other competing claims which may, at first, bear
a superficial resemblance to Yahweh's. Only in this
way, II Isaiah suggests, can Israel affirm the values
and beliefs that come from Yahweh, and reject those that
have their source in the claims of a human power such
as Babylon.

It is significant that II Isaiah is the only
writer in the Old Testament to use divine self-
predication in this setting, in which God's word stands
in such clear contrast to human response, on the one

hand, and human claims on the other. He is the only
writer to place statements such as "I am Yahweh" over
against Israel's anticipated response, "Thou art
Yahweh," and over against Babylon's pretentious claim
to divine power, "I am, and there is no one besides me."
Ezekiel perhaps comes closest to II Isaiah in this
respect, but he does not indicate so clearly that he
expects Israel to express her faith by acknowledging
Yahweh as her God, nor does he explore the claims to
divine status and power implicit in Babylon's assertion,
"I am." II Isaiah emphasizes the importance of divine
self-predication by seeing it in relation to the
response that it should evoke, even though Israel has
not yet given that response and may not be able to give
it for some time. He also emphasizes the importance of
Yahweh's self-predication by setting it over against
human claims to status and power, since these two forms
of self-predication represent competing claims to be
the source of meaning and value. In these ways II
Isaiah reveals that he has perceived more clearly than
previous writers the full significance of divine self-
predications such as "I am Yahweh."

The frequency with which II Isaiah uses formulas
of self-predication also gives some indication of the
importance that he attributes to this type of speech.
He uses "I am Yahweh" a total of eighteen times, fifteen
times in the form ani Yahweh, twice as anoki Yahweh,
and once as anoki anoki Yahweh.[60] He uses the more
general expression "I am God" only four times, once as
ani eloheka (with the suffix "your"), twice as ani el,
and once as anoki el.[61] As an especially distinctive
usage, II Isaiah employs "I am He" eight times, six
times in the form ani hu and twice in the longer form
anoki anoki hu.[62] This usage is especially significant

in light of the fact that the self-predication "I am He"
is so rare elsewhere in the Old Testament, occurring
only in Deut. 32:39. All together, II Isaiah uses
formulas of divine self-predication a total of thirty
times. In this respect II Isaiah is comparable to the
other sources that come from the time of the exile and
very probably from the situation of exile itself --
i.e., the P document, the Holiness Code, and Ezekiel.

A. "I am Yahweh"

In the earlier part of our study we treated "I am
Yahweh," "I am God," and "I am He" separately, examining
each form of self-predication as it occurred in specific
sources and then making comparisons among the three
forms. It will be helpful to follow a similar procedure
as we turn now to II Isaiah. We may look at each form
of self-predication separately, with special reference
to the type of passage in which it appears, the audience
that is addressed, and the themes with which the self-
predication is associated. As in the previous part of
our study, it will be especially important to ask
whether an example of divine self-predication is
associated with ideas that represent the themes of
"grace" and "law," singly or in combination with each
other.

1. Trial Scene: Yahweh and the Nations

In II Isaiah the formula "I am Yahweh" appears
for the first time as part of a trial scene (Is. 41:1-4)
in which Yahweh summons the peoples of the earth to
appear with him in court to determine who is guiding the
career of Cyrus, the "one from the east whom victory

meets at every step" (Is. 41:2). The purpose of this
type of trial scene is not to assign blame for wrongdoing, but to adjudicate between competing claims; in
modern terms, it would correspond more to a civil suit
than a criminal trial. The course of the trial makes
it clear that Yahweh, rather than the gods of other
nations, is really guiding the conquests of Cyrus.
Yahweh himself states the verdict in the form of the
self-predication "I am Yahweh," and his further designation of himself as "the first, and with the last" points
to his sovereignty over the entire course of history
(Is. 41:4). This first occurrence of the expression "I
am Yahweh" indicates, therefore, that II Isaiah is
thinking at this point of Yahweh as the sovereign Lord
of history who is guiding the victorious career of
Cyrus.

Within the dramatic setting of this trial scene,
the self-predication "I am Yahweh" is addressed to the
non-Jewish peoples of the world -- i.e., the Gentiles.
By using the formula in this way, II Isaiah wants to
articulate his own affirmations about Yahweh and present
them to the other nations of the world. At the same
time, however, it is important to recognize that his
immediate concern is to speak to his fellow exiles and
reassure them that Yahweh is indeed able to deliver them
from exile. He refers to Cyrus, not only to demonstrate
that Yahweh is guiding the current course of history,
but to indicate to the exiles that Yahweh has a purpose
which will soon affect them. He awards the verdict in
this trial to Yahweh, not only to show that the gods
of other peoples are "nothing" (cf. Is. 41:24), but to
remind the exiles that Yahweh is the sole God to whom
they look for deliverance. In these ways II Isaiah
indicates that the self-predication "I am Yahweh" is

clearly addressed to the Jewish exiles themselves as
well as the Gentile peoples of the world.

The formula "I am Yahweh" appears again in the
trial scene depicted in Is. 43:8-13, this time in the
longer form "I, I am Yahweh" (anoki anoki Yahweh, Is.
43:11). Again Yahweh summons the peoples of the earth
to appear in court to determine who controls the events
of history. In this passage II Isaiah states explicitly
some ideas that he had only implied in the earlier trial
scene -- Yahweh is the sole God in the world, and he is
Savior:

> Before me no god was formed,
> nor shall there be any after me.
> I, I am Yahweh,
> and besides me there is no savior.
>   (Is. 43:10c-11)

In this trial scene II Isaiah also indicates more
clearly than before that Yahweh's self-predication is
addressed to the exiles in Babylon as well as the
peoples of the world. He makes this clear by giving
the exiles themselves a prominent role as witnesses in
the trial. In this role they are asked to testify to
Yahweh's deeds in the past, probably at the time of the
Exodus from Egypt, when he "declared and saved and
proclaimed" and "there was no strange god" among them
(Is. 43:12). At the same time, through this activity
of testifying, the exiles will acquire a clearer
knowledge of Yahweh and a stronger faith in him (Is.
43:10). By appearing as witnesses for Yahweh, paradoxically, they will come to understand more fully the
meaning of his self-predication as it is addressed to
them in their situation of exile. They will perceive
more clearly that they are still called to fulfill
their responsibility as the covenant people, giving

testimony on behalf of Yahweh and growing in their own
knowledge, understanding, and faith. In this way II
Isaiah uses the divine self-predication to express the
theme of covenant obligation as well as grace. As an
indication of the importance that he attaches to the
themes in this passage, it is especially significant
that II Isaiah uses all three forms of self-predication
at this point -- "I am Yahweh," "I am God," and "I am
He."

The formulas of divine self-predication in Is.
41:4 and 43:11 appear in trial scenes between Yahweh
and the nations, in which Yahweh demonstrates that he,
rather than other gods, controls the course of history.
These scenes are addressed to the peoples of the world,
but they are also directed to the exiles in Babylon.
The self-predications convey the theme of Yahweh's
sovereignty over history, but they also express the idea
of grace -- i.e., Yahweh's intention to deliver Israel
from exile. The self-predication in Is. 43:11 also
appears in a trial scene that reminds Israel of her role
as the covenant people, even at a time when she
evidently felt that she had completely failed to live
up to the obligations of that role. In these respects
the trial scenes must be seen as complex passages that
have more than one audience and more than one major
theme.

2. Salvation Oracle

The formula "I am Yahweh" also appears in another
type of passage, the salvation oracle, which is addressed
more exclusively to Israel herself and is more immediately personal in tone. The position of the first
salvation oracle illustrates its relationship to the

trial scene between Yahweh and the nations. The trial
scene (Is. 41:1-4) has shown that Yahweh is acting
through the victorious career of Cyrus, with the
implication that he is working in this way to benefit
his own people. The following verses (Is. 41:5-7)
describe how the peoples of the world react to the trial
scene: they make a futile attempt to bolster their faith
in their own gods, even though these gods have now been
shown to be powerless. Then the salvation oracle (Is.
41:8-13) depicts the consequences of the trial scene as
they pertain to Israel. In this oracle Yahweh addresses
Israel directly, reassures her of his presence with her
now, and declares, in effect, that he is working through
Cyrus for the specific purpose of delivering Israel from
exile. This opening oracle illustrates clearly the
elements that are typical of this form of speech -- the
direct address to the recipient, the phrase of
reassurance ("fear not"), supporting clauses in the
present and the past, the promise of imminent help, and
the self-predication of the deity as the author of the
oracle:

> But you, Israel, my servant,
> > Jacob, whom I have chosen . . .
>
> fear not, for I am with you . . .
> > I have strengthened you,
> > I have helped you . . .
>
> those who strive against you
> > shall be as nothing
> > and shall perish . . .
>
> For I am Yahweh your God . . .
> > (Is. 41:8-13)[63]

The same formula of divine self-predication
appears in another salvation oracle (Is. 43:1-3), in
which again Yahweh assures Israel, in poetic language,

that he will deliver her from exile. Whereas the oracle
that we have just examined was closely related to a
trial scene, this oracle follows a rather lengthy
"reproach" (Is. 42:18-25) in which II Isaiah calls
attention to Israel's wrongdoing in the past as the
reason for the destruction of Jerusalem in 587 B.C.
II Isaiah stands in the tradition of the pre-exilic
prophets in the sense that he too reproaches Israel for
her grievous wrongs in the past. Pre-exilic prophets,
however, utilized the reproach as a basis for warning
of disaster to come, establishing a pattern of "reproach"
and "threat" (Scheltwort and Drohwort). II Isaiah
modifies this pattern by giving a reproach, oriented
toward the past (Is. 42:18-25), and then turning unexpectedly to the salvation oracle (Is. 43:1-3). In
this way he emphasizes the miraculous nature of Yahweh's
undeserved grace in restoring his people to their
homeland. Like the salvation oracle in Is. 41:8-13,
the present oracle concludes with a divine self-
predication that serves to authenticate and reaffirm
the assurances and promises of the oracle itself. The
appositives in the self-predication also have the effect
of emphasizing Yahweh's close relationship to Israel
and the gracious nature of his redemptive activity:
"For I am Yahweh your God, the Holy One of Israel,
your Savior" (Is. 43:3).

In these salvation oracles the formula "I am
Yahweh" is associated with ideas that continue and
extend the thought of the trial scenes between Yahweh
and the nations. The trial scenes were addressed to
the peoples of the world and also to Israel; the
salvation oracles are addressed directly to Israel,
with special reference to the situation of exile in
which Israel is now languishing. The trial scenes

expressed the theme of Yahweh's complete sovereignty
over history, with the implication that Yahweh was
planning to express this sovereignty by redeeming his
people Israel; the salvation oracles focus on the
redemption of Israel, depicting Yahweh's presence with
the exiles and the deliverance that he will soon provide.
The trial scenes, reflecting the background of a judicial
process, were formal in tone, especially in the divine
self-predications that announced the solemn verdict of
the trial (Is. 41:4; 43:13). The salvation oracles are
more immediately individual and personal in tone,
especially in the formulas in which Yahweh presents
himself to Israel as "your God," who does indeed "hold
your right hand," who is "your Savior" (Is. 41:13; 43:3).

3. Announcement of Salvation

The formula "I am Yahweh" also appears in Is. 43:
14-21, a passage that belongs to the category of the
"announcement of salvation." Like the salvation oracle,
the announcement of salvation proclaims the deliverance
that Yahweh will soon bring to his people Israel. The
typical salvation oracle, however, combines references
to the past, the present, and the future, at least to
the extent that the Hebrew verb forms can express
temporal references. Yahweh can say to Israel, for
example, "I have strengthened you, I have helped you,
I have upheld you with my victorious right hand" (Is.
41:10). Here the perfect tenses express a "past" time
in the sense that Yahweh has already made these unalter-
able decisions to help his people. Within the structure
of the salvation oracle, the references to the present
and the future then indicate the actual results that
follow from the decisions that Yahweh has made: "I am

with you . . . those who war against you shall be as
nothing at all" (Is. 41:10, 12). In contrast to this
complex treatment of temporal references in the
salvation oracle, the announcement of salvation
emphasizes the deliverance that Yahweh will bring in
the imminent future: "For your sake I will send to
Babylon and break down all the bars . . . I will make
a way in the wilderness and rivers in the desert" (Is.
43:14, 19). References to the past or the present in
the announcement of salvation seem to be more ancillary,
serving to support Yahweh's promise of deliverance in
the imminent future (cf. Is. 43:16-19).

The announcement of salvation in Is. 43:14-21
differs from the salvation oracles in two other ways.
It lacks the phrase of reassurance, "fear not," which
is characteristic of the pattern of the salvation
oracle. It also uses plural forms for "you" and "your,"
whereas the salvation oracles use the singular. It is
very possible that this difference between singular and
plural forms reflects a difference in background for the
two types of speech. The salvation oracle may derive
ultimately from the liturgical practice of the Jerusalem
temple, in which a priest, speaking in the name of
Yahweh, addressed an individual worshiper and assured
him that Yahweh had heard his lament. The announcement
of salvation seems to be addressed more directly to the
people of Israel, bringing them Yahweh's promise of
deliverance. It may have been formulated originally in
response to a communal lament, although it contains no
direct reference to the lament itself.

The verses in Is. 43:14-21 contain, in the
strictest sense, two announcements of salvation, each
introduced by the formula "thus says Yahweh" (Is. 43:
14, 16). Although each could stand by itself, their

presentation of complementary themes and expectations
suggests that they can be regarded as closely related
sections within a complex unit. The passage as a whole
refers to Yahweh's great act of deliverance in the past,
in the Exodus from Egypt (vss. 16-17), then to the
imminent liberation of the exiles from their captivity
in Babylon (vs. 14), and finally to their journey home-
ward through the "wilderness" separating Babylon from
Judah (vss. 19-20). The self-predication "I am Yahweh"
appears most directly as a way of confirming the promise
of liberation from captivity: "For your sake I will send
to Babylon and break down all the bars . . . I am
Yahweh, your Holy One, the Creator of Israel, your King"
(vss. 14-15). At the same time, in the context of the
whole passage, the phrase "I am Yahweh" also serves to
authenticate the two other themes. When God addresses
the exiles in the solemn and majestic formula of self-
predication, he is encouraging them to find new meaning
in the Exodus of long ago and fresh hope for imminent
deliverance and restoration to their homeland.

The three appositives that occur with the divine
name Yahweh in Is. 43:15 contribute significantly to
our understanding of the ideas and themes that II Isaiah
associates with the genre of divine self-predication:
"I am Yahweh, your Holy One, the Creator of Israel,
your King." When Yahweh presents himself to the exiles,
for example, he reminds them that he is their "Holy One."
This is a favorite expression of II Isaiah, which he
uses a number of times to describe Yahweh (Is. 40:25;
41:14, 16, 20; 43:3, 14, 15; 45:11; 47:4; 48:17; 49:7;
54:5; 55:5). Originally the idea of "holiness" may have
signified the "separation" between God and man, with
special reference to the distinctive qualities and
attributes that God has because he is God and not man.[64]

II Isaiah, however, almost always uses the expression
"Holy One" with some modifier that emphasizes the close
relationship that Yahweh has established with Israel.
Thus he speaks of Yahweh as "the Holy One of Israel,"
"your Holy One," or "his Holy One." In a similar way
he almost always links "Holy One" with "Yahweh," the
proper name of the God of Israel, and he frequently
links the expression also with the titles "Redeemer" or
"Savior," terms which depict Yahweh's role in delivering
his people from exile.

When II Isaiah speaks of Yahweh as the "Holy
One," he usually expresses the redemptive activity that
Yahweh undertakes in delivering his people from exile
in Babylon. He emphasizes, that is, the closeness or
presence of Yahweh to his people rather than his remote-
ness from them. At the same time, II Isaiah also seems
to be aware that the holiness of Yahweh involves the
uniqueness of his being and the transcendence of his
nature over all creation. As the Holy One, for example,
Yahweh is the incomparable Creator of all things (Is. 40:
25), and as the Holy One of Israel he teaches Israel to
live according to his commandments (Is. 48:17). As the
Holy One, Yahweh is the transcendent creator and
teacher; at the same time, paradoxically, he is the
Holy One who comes to his people and delivers them from
exile. The ways in which II Isaiah treats the theme of
God's holiness virtually form a commentary on a verse
in Hosea, some two centuries previously:

> for I am God and not man,
> > the Holy One in your midst,
> > and I will not come to destroy.
> > > (Hos. 11:9)

The self-predication of Yahweh in Is. 43:15 is
also associated with the ideas that Yahweh is the

Creator and the King of Israel. When II Isaiah speaks
of Yahweh as Creator, he seems to have in mind three
events or three times in which Yahweh exercised his
power to bring new realities into being. He thinks
first of the "original" creation when Yahweh made all
things in the universe (Is. 40:12, 25-26, 28; 42:5;
44:24, 27; 45:7, 12, 18; 48:13; 51:9-10, 13, 15-16).
More specifically, he thinks also of Yahweh as the
Creator of Israel (Is. 43:1; 44:2, 21, 24; 51:13; 54:5).
At this point it is very likely that II Isaiah is
thinking of the Exodus from Egypt as the redemptive
event through which Yahweh "created," "formed," or
"made" his people, calling them into being and giving
them an existence as a people that they had not enjoyed
before (cf. Is. 46:3; 48:8). Yahweh's work as Creator
merged with his work as Redeemer, so that in delivering
his people from bondage in Egypt he "created" them as a
new people, his special possession among all the peoples
of the earth (cf. Ex. 19:5). Indeed, whenever II Isaiah
speaks of Yahweh as Creator of Israel, he indicates in
the context that he is transferring the theme of
redemption from the "first" Exodus to the "second"
Exodus -- i.e., from the original deliverance from
bondage in Egypt to the imminent deliverance from
captivity in Babylon. In turn, this reference to the
anticipated deliverance from Babylon becomes the third
way in which II Isaiah speaks of Yahweh as Creator.
In "doing" this, Yahweh will be "creating" it (cf. Is.
41:20); he will bring about "new things," which "are
created now, not long ago" (Is. 48:6-7). Once again,
II Isaiah freely utilizes the vocabulary of creation
to depict an event of redemption in history.

In a similar way II Isaiah associates the self-
predication of Yahweh in Is. 43:15 with the assertion

that Yahweh is the King of Israel. Near the very
beginning of his writing, in Is. 40:3-5, he introduced
the concept of the kingship of Yahweh by the announcement that it was time to prepare a highway in the desert
so that Yahweh could return to Zion, in the same way as
a road was made level and smooth before a human monarch
traveled over it. II Isaiah also alludes to the concept
elsewhere when he proclaims that Yahweh's arm "rules"
for him (Is. 40:10) and that Yahweh himself "reigns" or
"is king" (Is. 52:7). More directly, he describes
Yahweh as "King of Jacob" (Is. 41:21) and "King of
Israel" (Is. 44:6). In both passages he links the
concept of kingship with the proper name Yahweh; more
specifically, he connects the concept with the assertion
of Yahweh's uniqueness over against other gods and with
the affirmation of his sovereignty over history. As
King, Yahweh is also the Redeemer of Israel who reassures his people that they will receive the salvation
which he has promised (Is. 44:6).[65]

Our study of the formula "I am Yahweh" in earlier
Old Testament sources indicated that it was frequently
connected with the themes of both grace and law -- i.e.,
the Exodus deliverance from Egypt and the religious and
ethical obligations of the Sinai covenant. II Isaiah's
use of the formula in Is. 43:15 suggests that he too is
associating it with both grace and law. In the announcement of salvation, of course, he wishes to emphasize
that Yahweh will soon deliver his people from captivity,
just as he delivered them long ago in the Exodus from
Egypt. In this respect the self-predication "I am
Yahweh" serves to express primarily the theme of grace.
At the same time, however, II Isaiah links the name
Yahweh with appositives which reinforce the affirmation
that Yahweh is Lord of the covenant as well as Redeemer:

"I am Yahweh, your Holy One, the Creator of Israel, your King." As Holy One, Yahweh redeems his people, and he also leads them in the way they should go. As Creator of Israel, he brought his people into being by delivering them from captivity in Egypt; it may be part of the same complex of thought that in the same role he formalized his relationship with the people by giving them the Sinai covenant. As King of Israel, Yahweh delivered Israel from Egypt, revealed himself to Moses, and gave the law through Moses (cf. Num. 23:20-24; Deut. 33:2-5). We receive the impression that II Isaiah has selected these appositives very carefully as a way of emphasizing that Yahweh will soon redeem the exiles from captivity, and as a way of indicating, at the same time, that Yahweh still expects his people to fulfill their religious and ethical obligations under the covenant.

We can appreciate more fully the significance of the self-predication in Is. 43:15 if we compare its terms and motifs with those of the group of psalms known as the Enthronement Psalms. These refer especially to Yahweh in his role as King (Ps. 93:1; 95:3; 96:10; 97:1; 98:6; 99:1; 145:1). A number of them also refer to Yahweh's work in creating the world (Ps. 93:3-4; 95:4-6; 96:5; 98:7-8). In a similar way, many of them indicate directly or indirectly that Yahweh is holy (Ps. 93:5; 96:9; 97:12; 98:1; 99:3; 145:21). In these ways the Enthronement Psalms echo virtually the same ideas that II Isaiah expresses as appositives to the name Yahweh in Is. 43:15; "I am Yahweh, your Holy One, the Creator of Israel, your King." More importantly, the Enthronement Psalms also depict Yahweh as the ultimate source of both grace and law. He is the God who delivers and saves (Ps. 95:1; 96:2-3; 98:1-3; 99:6; 145:4-19), and

he is also the God who gives statutes and laws that he
wishes for his people to follow (Ps. 95:7-11; 96:13;
97:10-12; 98:9; 99:7-8; 145:20). These close parallels
between the Enthronement Psalms and the formula of self-
predication in Is. 43:15 suggest that II Isaiah
anticipated continued covenant obligation as well as
imminent deliverance for the exiles, even if the
circumstances of his situation in Babylon led him to
emphasize the theme of deliverance when he employed the
formula of divine self-predication.

4. Hymn of Self-Praise

We may turn now to the use of the expression "I
am Yahweh" in another type of speech, the hymn of self-
praise, in which Yahweh speaks in the first person and
extols the qualities and attributes that he possesses
in a unique sense. Some years ago Hugo Gressmann, in
his classic study of literary forms in II Isaiah, called
attention to the "hymnic expansion" of the formula "I am
Yahweh," in which Yahweh praised himself in the first
person. Noting that this expansion resulted in a type
of speech that was unique to II Isaiah in the Old
Testament, he suggested that the prophet was dependent
at this point on Babylonian models.[66] More recently,
H.-M. Dion has analyzed in greater detail this "hymn to
oneself" in which "Yahweh sings, in a certain manner, a
hymn to his own glory."[67] Dion emphasized that this
type of hymn is primarily "descriptive" rather than
"narrative," depicting Yahweh's qualities in a "univer-
salizing" manner rather than stressing the narrative
recital of his benevolent deeds. He argued that this
hymn readily incorporates certain forms of speech which
in themselves are not hymnic, such as the "formula of

exclusiveness" ("apart from me, there is no God"), the
"formula of incomparability" ("there is no other like
me"), and the "formula of self-presentation" ("I am
Yahweh"). With the help of ancient texts, Dion
developed the view that the hymn of self-praise on the
part of a deity was a Sumerian literary genre dating
from a time before the end of the third millennium;
he argued further that this genre survived, and became
known to II Isaiah, in the form of the lavish praises
that the human monarchs of the Near East addressed to
themselves at the beginning of royal inscriptions.
When II Isaiah took over the form, Dion notes, he
modified it in several respects: the content of the
hymn became strictly monotheistic, the hymn included
some narration of Yahweh's deeds as well as description
of his attributes, and the hymn combined the praise of
Yahweh with expressions of his concern for the salvation
of his people.[68]

        Since II Isaiah sometimes composes "mixed"
passages that combine elements from different types of
form critical units, we may note first how the theme of
self-praise can appear in passages which are not in
themselves hymns of self-praise. In Is. 42:8, for
example, Yahweh says, "I am Yahweh, that is my name;
my glory I give to no other, nor my praise to graven
images." Here the formula of divine self-predication
is combined with the motifs of exclusiveness and self-
praise. The whole passage in Is. 42:5-9, however, puts
its main emphasis on the charge that Yahweh gives to
Israel, to be "a covenant to the people, a light to the
nations" (Is. 42:6). The theme of Yahweh's self-praise
is not presented for its own sake but as a way of high-
lighting Yahweh's status as the sole God who can indeed
give his people a task on the scene of world history.

In a similar way the motif of self-praise appears in
Is. 43:11 and Is. 45:5-7. In the first instance it
occurs within a trial scene between Yahweh and the
nations, and in the second passage it occurs in the
context of Yahweh's address to Cyrus of Persia. In
both passages the theme of self-praise is presented,
not for its own sake, but as a way of reinforcing the
main emphasis of the passage. It is significant that
all these examples of self-praise (Is. 42:8; 43:11;
45:5-7) occur in passages that deal with the relationship between Yahweh and other nations of the world; for
II Isaiah, that is, the motif of Yahweh's self-praise
incorporates an implicit polemic against the other gods
of the world, who do not have the status or being of
Yahweh himself.

We may also look briefly at Is. 44:6-8, a passage
that does illustrate the hymn of self-praise although
it lacks the formula "I am Yahweh." In these verses
the theme of self-praise is the main emphasis of the
passage. The prophetic messenger formula ("thus says
Yahweh") seems to replace the formula of divine self-
predication ("I am Yahweh"), but then the passage
presents the theme of exclusiveness ("I am the first
and I am the last; besides me there is no god") and the
theme of incomparability ("who is like me?"). In the
sense that these themes all reinforce the idea of self-
praise, which is presented for its own sake as the main
idea of the passage, these verses may be regarded as an
example of the hymn of self-praise. At the same time,
the passage incorporates elements from the trial scene
between Yahweh and the nations ("have I not told you
from of old and declared it? and you are my witnesses!") and also elements from the salvation oracle
("fear not, nor be afraid"). As the theme of self-

praise may reinforce the main idea in other types of passages, here certain elements from other genres have a supporting role in a hymn of self-praise.

The hymn of self-praise in Is. 44:24-28 illustrates many of the features that we have noticed. It opens with the messenger formula ("thus says Yahweh") and then continues almost immediately with the formula of self-predication ("I am Yahweh"). The structure of the hymn makes it especially clear that this affirmation "I am Yahweh" is the central idea of the poem, since the passage continues, in a predominantly participial style, to present a series of subordinate points which describe Yahweh's activities and give substance to the meaning of his self-predication. As he presents himself to the Jewish exiles, therefore, Yahweh reminds them that he created all things (Is. 44:24, 27), that he frustrates the intentions of the wise men of Babylon (or possibly the wise men of Egypt at the time of the Exodus, Is. 44:25), that he confirms the words of his prophets (Is. 44:26), and that he plans to work through Cyrus for the ultimate goal of rebuilding Jerusalem and Judah (Is. 44:26, 28). These references to Yahweh's activity in creation and in history function to support the central theme of the poem, the divine self-predication itself. At the same time, by describing the accomplishments in which Yahweh takes pride, they illustrate how the self-predication "I am Yahweh" can become the focal point of a hymn of self-praise.

We noticed earlier that the motif of self-praise contains an implicit polemic against the other gods of the world, who do not have the status or nature of Yahweh himself (Is. 42:8; 43:11; 45:5-7). In this sense Yahweh praises himself because he alone can be the object of his praise. In the present passage, Is. 44:24-28,

we perceive another important aspect of the idea of
self-praise. Here Yahweh engages in self-praise, not
so much to contrast himself with other gods, as to
reassure the exiles in Babylon that he does exist, he
can deliver them from exile, and he will indeed do so
in the near future. Yahweh's self-praise reaches out
beyond itself, as it were, to become an integral factor
in his relationship with his people. As II Isaiah
indicates at the beginning of his poem, Yahweh addresses
his people as "your Redeemer, who formed you from the
womb" (Is. 44:24). In this respect the purpose of the
hymn of self-praise overlaps with that of the disputation, a type of passage in which Yahweh contends with
the exiles' sense of despair and seeks to give them new
hope for the future.

        In a very similar manner the hymn of self-praise
in Is. 45:18-19 also addresses the profound discouragement of the exiles and reminds them of Yahweh's nature
and activities with the intention of instilling new
hope for the future. In several respects this hymn
corresponds closely to the one in Is. 44:24-28 -- it
begins with the messenger formula ("thus says Yahweh"),
it has its focal point in the divine self-predication
("I am Yahweh"), it employs the participial style
("creating the heavens . . . forming the earth"), it
presents the theme of the exclusiveness of Yahweh
("there is no other"), and it refers to Yahweh's deeds
in creation (Is. 45:18) and in history (Is. 45:19) as
a way of supporting and illuminating the divine self-
predication rather than vice versa. These similarities
in content and structure with Is. 44:24-28 indicate
that Is. 45:18-19 may also be regarded as an example of
the hymn of self-praise.

In this hymn the use of the term "chaos" (tohu)
is especially noteworthy because it forms a transitional
link between Yahweh's activity in creation and his
activity in history. The statement that Yahweh did not
create the world "a chaos" (Is. 45:18) implies that he
created it to be a place of purpose, order, and meaning,
eminently suitable for human life; in a similar way,
the assertion that he did not tell the people of Israel
to seek him "in chaos" (Is. 45:19) means that he did
reveal himself to them in a clear, intelligible, and
meaningful way. At this point II Isaiah is probably
thinking of the preaching of the pre-exilic prophets,
who declared Yahweh's will in open, public proclamation,
rather than "in secret" (Is. 45:19).[69] This double use
of the word "chaos" points to the inner consistency of
Yahweh's character, indicating that he reveals himself
in history as an expression of the same goals and
purposes for which he originally created the world.
This use of "chaos" is parallel to the use of the term
"sea" in Is. 51:10, which in a very similar way links
Yahweh's activity in creation (his victory over the
"sea") with his activity in history (leading his people
through the "sea" at the time of the Exodus from Egypt).
For our present study it is significant that each use
of the term "chaos" -- i.e., each assertion that Yahweh
acted in a meaningful, intelligible manner, whether in
creation or in historical revelation -- is followed
closely by the self-predication "I am Yahweh." In this
way the assertions about the nature and purpose of
Yahweh's activity help to illumine the meaning of his
self-predications, which are the focal points in this
hymn of self-praise.

It is also significant for our present study that
Is. 45:19 refers to Yahweh's word to Israel as it was

communicated to her by the pre-exilic prophets. Yahweh
did not speak "in secret," nor did he tell Israel to
seek him "in chaos." He revealed his will through his
prophets, who spoke clearly and openly in the streets
and the market-places and interpreted his will as it
related to Israel's historical situation. Muilenburg's
comment on this verse indicates that Yahweh's word to
Israel also recalls his covenant with her at the time
of Moses: "The JE accounts of the covenant and its
demands are an effective commentary on the prophet's
words, and the whole of Hebrew prophecy documents
them."[70] As Is. 45:19 refers in the first instance to
the preaching of the pre-exilic prophets, it also refers
at the same time to the obligations of the Sinai
covenant, which so often formed the basis for reflection
and analysis on the part of the prophets. In this verse,
therefore, the expression "I am Yahweh" is associated
with the theme of covenant obligation as well as the
theme of grace. It reminds Israel of the grace that
Yahweh has shown and will continue to show, and it also
recalls the covenant obligations that Yahweh presented
to Israel at Sinai and that he still expects her to
fulfill.

The terms that II Isaiah uses in the self-
predication at the close of this passage lend support
to the view that he is thinking in terms of covenant
obligation as well as grace. This self-predication
could be translated literally, "I am Yahweh, speaking
righteousness, declaring what is right" (Is. 45:19).
The word "righteousness" here represents tsedeq, an
important term which II Isaiah uses in a variety of
contexts. At one point he uses it of the ethical or
spiritual righteousness that the people attain through
obeying Yahweh's law (Is. 51:7). More typically,

however, he uses tsedeq of some action by which Yahweh
himself "makes things right" for his people by helping
them or delivering them from distress. This is the case
in Is. 45:8; 51:1; and 51:5; in all of these passages
tsedeq could be translated "deliverance," and in the
first and third of these passages it stands in poetic
parallelism with yesha', "salvation." The idea that
tsedeq represents some action of Yahweh for the benefit
of his people is present also in Is. 41:2, 10; 42:6, 21;
45:13. In Is. 41:2 and 41:10 the word actually represents the "victory" that Yahweh wins for his people; in
Is. 41:2 this victory benefits Cyrus of Persia directly,
and thus Israel indirectly. Most of these examples
indicate, therefore, that II Isaiah uses tsedeq to
represent some aspect of the theme of grace, especially
as it finds expression in an action that Yahweh undertakes, on his own initiative, to benefit his people in
their current historical situation.

    As Yahweh speaks "righteousness" in Is. 45:19,
he also declares "what is right." These last words
represent the term mesharim, which occurs only here in
II Isaiah's writings. It is related to the stem yashar,
which as a verb means "be straight" and as an adjective
means "straight, just, upright." In its occurrences
outside of II Isaiah, mesharim can mean the "upright-
ness" or "right" that the righteous person is to know
or follow (Is. 26:7; 33:15; Prov. 1:3; 2:9; 8:6; 23:16).
It can also be used with reference to God's activity to
denote the "right" or "equity" with which he judges the
world or individual persons (Ps. 9:9; 17:2; 75:3;
96:10; 98:9). When Yahweh declares "what is right," he
is declaring the expectations that he places before his
people and the norms by which he judges them. It seems
very likely, therefore, that "what is right" represents

the theme of covenant obligation, just as the term
"righteousness" represents the theme of grace. For the
interpretation of II Isaiah, it is especially important
that both themes are associated with the formula of
divine self-predication in Is. 45:19: "I am Yahweh,
speaking righteousness, declaring what is right."[71]

5. Disputation with Israel

The phrase "I am Yahweh" also appears in another
type of speech, the disputation, in which II Isaiah
depicts Yahweh as seeking to disprove the assertion of
the exiles that they had no hope of returning to their
homeland. Of the various forms of speech that II Isaiah
employs, perhaps the disputation has the most tendency
to resemble other forms or incorporate motifs from other
forms. Joachim Begrich, for instance, noted that the
disputation was related to the trial speeches, and he
also observed that it sometimes incorporated themes from
Israel's hymns.[72] Claus Westermann also noted the
similarity that the disputation showed to the trial
scenes and the hymns. In his analysis of the disputation
in Is. 40:12-31, he argued specifically that the
"descriptive psalm of praise" (beschreibende Lobpsalm)
underlies the passage as a whole. In his discussion of
Is. 49:14-26 he developed the view that the passage is
an intentional composition combining two forms of
speech, the disputation and the announcement of
salvation (which in part here approximates the salvation
oracle).[73] We could notice in addition that the
complaint of the exiles, to which the disputation is
directed, echoes the themes of the lament -- for
example, "Yahweh has forsaken me, my Lord has forgotten
me" (Is. 49:14). As a form of speech, the disputation

evidently acted as a magnet, attracting elements from
other types of speech. In II Isaiah, the distinguishing
characteristic of the disputations is that the prophet's
primary purpose in these passages is to overcome the
mood of despair into which his fellow exiles have
fallen. He seeks to counter their arguments that Yahweh
has abandoned them in Babylon -- that he can not, or
will not, lead them back to Israel.

The disputation in Is. 49:14-26 contains three
complaints or laments on the part of the Jewish exiles:
they feel abandoned by Yahweh (vs. 14), they are like a
barren woman, with no hope of descendants to repopulate
the land of Israel (vs. 21), and they are captives of a
mighty empire, Babylon, with no hope of being rescued
(vs. 24). II Isaiah presents each lament in its own
individual form: direct lament (vs. 14), reflection from
the standpoint of the future (vs. 21), and rhetorical
question (vs. 24). The first lament seems to imply that
Yahweh will not help the exiles, while the second two
seem to suggest that he can not help them. The two
thoughts are closely related, and II Isaiah responds to
them both, as he does in the very similar passage in
Is. 40:27-31. He reassures the exiles that Yahweh does
not forget them (Is. 49:14-18), that their descendants
will again fill the land of Israel (Is. 49:19-23), and
that they will indeed be set free from their captivity
in Babylon (Is. 49:24-26). The first promise ends with
a solemn oath: "as I live, says Yahweh . . ." (vs. 18).
The second and third promises end with solemn self-
predications: "you will know that I am Yahweh" (vs. 23),
and "all flesh shall know that I am Yahweh" (vs. 26).
The parallelism between the oath and the formula of
self-predication emphasizes the seriousness and
solemnity of the self-predication "I am Yahweh."

It is especially significant that II Isaiah uses
the introductory statement "you (they) shall know that
. . ." before the self-predication "I am Yahweh" in Is.
49:23, 26. As we saw earlier, the prophet Ezekiel
almost always used this introductory statement before
the divine self-predication, with the result that the
link between the introductory statement and the self-
predication became especially characteristic of this
prophet. We also noted Zimmerli's belief that this
link served to express the view that Yahweh initiated
the history of his people by revealing himself to them,
and then continued to work through their history so
that they would know him more fully. For Israel, this
understanding of history meant that knowing the meaning
of the expression "I am Yahweh" was both the beginning
and the goal of her history.[74] II Isaiah may well have
a similar view in mind when he links the introductory
statement with the self-predication "I am Yahweh." He
wants to remind his fellow exiles that the real goal of
their history is not simply to return to their homeland,
as important as that is in itself, but to know more
fully the meaning of the divine self-predication. Their
history as a people began with God's revelation of himself, "I am Yahweh," and it always moves toward the goal
of understanding this revelation more completely.
Liberation from captivity and restoration from exile
will represent important stages along the way to this
goal of knowing Yahweh as he has revealed himself to
his people.

It may also be significant that these two verses
(Is. 49:23, 26) represent the only occasions on which
II Isaiah employed the introductory statement "you (they)
shall know that . . ." before the self-predication "I am
Yahweh" in addressing his fellow exiles in Babylon. The

fact that he uses the combination only here may well be
a way of emphasizing the importance of his message in
this passage. The disputation as a whole promises that
Yahweh will indeed redeem his people; more specifically,
the formula "I am Yahweh" is associated here with the
theme of divine grace and deliverance. It is also
possible, however, that some of the people in II Isaiah's
audience would have been familiar with the preaching or
writings of Ezekiel. These people would have known
that Ezekiel almost always used the solemn introductory
statement before the divine self-predication, and they
would have known too that Ezekiel clearly connected the
self-predication with the theme of covenant obligation
as well as divine grace. For these people, at least,
the statement "you shall know that I am Yahweh" could
imply not only that Yahweh would deliver his people,
but that he also looked forward to a renewed relationship with them in which they would seek to fulfill their
covenant obligations.

      The other disputation in which II Isaiah uses
the formula "I am Yahweh" appears in Is. 51:9-52:2.
The passage begins with a lament, in which the exiles
call upon Yahweh to "awake" and do something to help
them (Is. 51:9). They remind Yahweh that he was able
to perform wonderful deeds in the past, in creating the
world (vss. 9b-10a) and in setting his people free at
the time of the Exodus from Egypt (vs. 10b). The clear
implication of their lament is that they want Yahweh to
help them now, just as he performed marvelous deeds in
the past. Yahweh's response to this lament begins in
Is. 51:12 and continues to the end of the passage. His
reply begins with a self-predication of the type "I am
He" (here with repetition for emphasis and solemnity,
anoki anoki hu) and then continues with the more familiar

"I am Yahweh" (Is. 51:15). The reply picks up the theme
that Yahweh is indeed the creator and sustainer of the
world (Is. 51:13, 15-16). In a way that is especially
characteristic of his thought, II Isaiah utilizes this
theme to support his assertion that Yahweh is the
powerful God who can and will redeem his people (vss.
12-16). In this respect the argument of the disputation
replies directly to the lament that it has quoted. On
a linguistic level the disputation also responds to the
lament by repeating some of its terms and redirecting
them to the exiles themselves. The lament had opened
by asking Yahweh to "awake" ('ur) and put on "strength"
('oz); the disputation closes by directing these same
words back to the exiles as a way of reminding them
that they are the ones who should "awake" and start to
do something, now that they have the assurance of
Yahweh's intervention in their history (Is. 51:9; 52:1).
In its intensive-reflexive form the same verb occurs in
the central part of the disputation as a way of reminding the exiles that they should "rouse themselves" and
take hope, now that their time of punishment is over
(Is. 51:17).

In this disputation it is especially significant
that the self-predication "I am Yahweh" is closely
linked with the covenant formula "you are my people":

> For I am Yahweh your God,
> > who stirs up the sea so that
> > > its waves roar . . .
> > stretching out the heavens
> > > and laying the foundations of the earth,
> > > and saying to Zion, "You are my people."
> > > > (Is. 51:15-16)

This is the only passage in which II Isaiah links the
formula "I am Yahweh" with the covenant formula;

indeed, it is the only place where he uses the terminology of the covenant formula at all, although verses
such as Is. 43:20-21 and 51:4 seem to reflect the
language of this formula. In its basic form the
covenant formula seems to have been "I will be your God,
and you shall be my people" (Jer. 7:23). As this
example from Jeremiah indicates, the formula had
reference to the Sinai covenant, which occurred shortly
after the Exodus deliverance from Egypt (Jer. 7:22) and
was contingent on the people"s obedience to the commandments (Jer. 7:23). In connecting the divine self-
predication with the covenant formula, therefore, II
Isaiah is associating the expression "I am Yahweh" with
the theme of the covenant obligation that Israel is to
accept as well as the motif of the grace that Yahweh
shows in delivering the people from exile. To understand more fully the significance of this link between
the divine self-predication and the covenant formula,
we may look briefly at the source of each and ask
whether they are combined elsewhere in Old Testament
writings.

     The original setting for the self-predication
"I am Yahweh" was probably God's revelation of himself
to Moses. This setting is implied by the early narrative
sources (J and E), and it is supported by Hosea, the
Holiness Code, the priestly document, and Ezekiel. It
is true, as we saw earlier, that the early narrative
sources indicate that God was revealing himself in a
way that would affect the people of Israel, the pharaoh
of Egypt, and even the people of Egypt. In this sense
God's revelation to Moses was intended to reach out
beyond itself to affect others. Yet the revelation
itself -- "I am Yahweh" -- was directed in the first
instance to Moses. It signified the divine self-
disclosure to an individual person.

The covenant formula, in contrast, is addressed
to the community of Israel. When God promises "I will
be your God and you will be my people," he is addressing
the people as a corporate whole. The covenant formula,
therefore, must have had its original setting in a
scene of covenant-making involving Yahweh and Israel.
In this respect it differs from the phrase "I am Yahweh,"
which originated in a scene of revelation to an individual person. This difference in origin raises the
question whether the two formulas ever came together in
the same context, as they do in Is. 51:15-16.

It is evident that the divine self-predication
occurs many times by itself, apart from the covenant
formula, and the covenant formula occurs a number of
times apart from the self-predication.[75] At a number
of points, however, they come together in Old Testament
tradition. A typical example occurs in Yahweh's address
to Moses as it was formulated in the P document:

> I am Yahweh, and I will bring you out
> from under the burdens of the Egyptians
> . . . and I will take you for my people,
> and I will be your God; and you shall
> know that I am Yahweh your God, who has
> brought you out from under the burdens
> of the Egyptians.
>
> (Ex. 6:6-7)

In this passage the divine self-predication, the
reference to the Exodus from Egypt, and the covenant
formula are all closely connected; the self-predication,
followed directly by the reference to the Exodus, occurs
before and after the covenant formula. This position
of the covenant formula, in turn, makes it clear that
the formula refers specifically to the Sinai covenant,
which followed very shortly after the Exodus. The fact

that the covenant formula is given before the reference
to the entry into Canaan (vs. 8) confirms that it
anticipates and depicts the Sinai covenant. Several
other passages, also from the P document, have their
setting within the priestly instructions and ordinances
delivered at Mt. Sinai. As in Ex. 6:6-7, they also
combine the self-predication "I am Yahweh" with a
reference to the Exodus and a statement of covenant
relationship (cf. Ex. 29:44-46; Lev. 11:44-45; Num.
15:40-41). It is interesting that these passages all
use a purpose construction as a succinct variant of
the covenant formula -- for example, "I am Yahweh your
God, who brought you out of the land of Egypt, to be
your God: I am Yahweh your God" (Num. 15:41). This
way of presenting the covenant formula illustrates
that it is closely related to the Exodus and confirms,
at the same time, that it refers to the Sinai covenant.

In a similar way several passages from the
Holiness Code link the divine self-predication "I am
Yahweh" with a reference to the Exodus from Egypt and
a statement of the covenant formula. This formula may
appear in the short form, "to be your God," indicating
the purpose of the Exodus and showing the close relationship between the Exodus and the Sinai covenant
(cf. Lev. 22:32-33; 25:38). Or the formula may appear
in an expanded form, "And I will walk among you, and
will be your God, and you shall be my people" (Lev.
26:12). In either case these passages illustrate how
closely "I am Yahweh" may be associated with a reference
to the Exodus and a presentation of the covenant
formula. As it closes, the Holiness Code also trans-
poses these themes into a higher key by directing them
specifically to the situation of the sixth century B.C.
This final chapter of the Holiness Code depicts the

situation of exile into which Yahweh will send his
faithless people -- or the exile into which he has
already sent them, from the standpoint of the author
of the Holiness Code, sometime after 597 B.C. (cf. Lev.
26:27-33). The chapter goes on to promise mercy if
the exiles repent (Lev. 26:40-41), and then it gives
the assurance that Yahweh will indeed remember his
covenant:

> Yet for all that, when they are in the
> land of their enemies, I will not spurn
> them, neither will I abhor them so as to
> destroy them utterly and break my covenant
> with them; for I am Yahweh their God;
> but I will for their sake remember the
> covenant with their forefathers, whom
> I brought forth out of the land of Egypt
> in the sight of the nations, that I might
> be their God: I am Yahweh.
>
> (Lev. 26:44-45)

The new theme in this passage is that the Exodus
from Egypt now serves as a model for the expectation of
restoration from exile, as Yahweh remembers the Sinai
covenant and promises now not to break it. The fact
that Yahweh does promise to maintain the Sinai covenant
means that he still regards the exiles as his people
and so provides them with the hope that at some point
he will bring them back from exile. The writer of the
passage does not want to raise false hopes among the
exiles. He does not try to indicate when Yahweh will
bring them back, and he actually alludes to the idea of
restoration only in a very indirect manner. But he
does make it clear that Yahweh's faithfulness to the
Sinai covenant provides a genuine basis of hope for
those in exile. In this way the Sinai covenant serves

to incorporate the theme of divine grace as well as
"the statutes and ordinances and laws" that the people
are to accept (Lev. 26:46).

In a very similar way Jeremiah links the divine
self-predication with the covenant formula in a passage
that refers to the restoration of the exiles to their
homeland. Jeremiah speaks of the exiles as "good figs,"
with whom lies the hope for the future, in contrast to
the "bad figs," the king of Judah and his princes who
remained behind after the deportation of 597 B.C. As
Jeremiah looks to the future, he thinks in terms of a
promise that Yahweh makes to restore the exiles: "I will
set my eyes upon them for good, and I will bring them
back to this land . . . I will give them a heart to
know that I am Yahweh; and they shall be my people and
I will be their God, for they shall return to me with
their whole heart" (Jer. 24:6-7). The expression "I am
Yahweh" occurs in close conjunction with the promises
of the covenant formula, and the assertion that the
exiles themselves will "return" to Yahweh "with their
whole heart" implies that they will bring a new sense
of commitment and obedience to the covenant that Yahweh
promises.

This is the only passage in which Jeremiah
combines the self-predication "I am Yahweh" with the
covenant formula. For two reasons, however, his other
citations of the formula are significant. They indicate,
first, that he regarded the covenant formula as a
specific reference to the Sinai covenant, with its
theme of covenant obligation on the part of Israel.
In 7:22-23, for example, Jeremiah represents Yahweh as
declaring, "For in the day that I brought them out of
the land of Egypt . . . this command I gave them,
'Obey my voice, and I will be your God, and you shall

be my people; and walk in all the way that I command
you, that it may be well with you'" (cf. Jer. 11:3-5).
Jeremiah's citations of the covenant formula also
illustrate, secondly, how he projected this idea into
the future to depict the renewal of the covenant
relationship that would accompany the restoration of
the captives from their exile in Babylon (Jer. 30:22;
31:1, 33; 32:38). Sometimes these references express
the gracious action of Yahweh in restoring his people
from exile (Jer. 30:22; 31:1); sometimes, as in Jer.
24:6-7, they also depict the new sense of moral and
spiritual commitment with which the people will respond
to Yahweh's gracious act of redemption (Jer. 31:33;
32:38).

In the same historical situation the prophet
Ezekiel employs the phrase "I am Yahweh" in connection
with the covenant formula in passages that promise
restoration of the exiles from Babylon (Ezek. 34:25-31;
36:22-32; 37:24-28). Like Jeremiah, Ezekiel evidently
believes that it will be these exiles who will return
to Judah and provide the moral and spiritual leadership
that the country so desperately needs. Even more
explicitly than Jeremiah, Ezekiel expresses the belief
that those who accept Yahweh's promise of a new covenant
will respond with a new sense of obedience to the
"statutes" and "ordinances" that the covenant will
include (cf. Ezek. 36:27; 37:24). It is also significant that Ezekiel describes the new covenant as an
"everlasting covenant" (berith 'olam, Ezek. 37:26).
Jeremiah used the same phrase in speaking of the new
covenant that Yahweh would make (Jer. 32:40); and the
P document, within the context of the original Sinai
covenant, could also speak of sabbath observance as an
"everlasting covenant" (berith 'olam, Ex. 31:16). In

Old Testament tradition this phrase "everlasting
covenant" is perhaps associated more closely with the
covenant that Yahweh made with David and his descendants
on the throne (for berith 'olam, cf. II Sam. 23:5; for
similar terminology, cf. also Ps. 89:29; II Sam. 7:16).
It would seem that Ezekiel, Jeremiah, and the priestly
writer all appropriate the phrase "everlasting covenant"
for the Sinai covenant, or the anticipated renewal of
the Sinai covenant, as a way of emphasizing that this
covenant will have a secure foundation in Yahweh's
gracious promises to his people. The new covenant,
like the original Sinai covenant, will entail covenant
obligation on the part of the people; but it can also
be described accurately as an "everlasting covenant"
because it will have its source in Yahweh's gracious
promises and redemptive activity.

Because II Isaiah links the phrase "I am Yahweh"
with the covenant formula in Is. 51:15-16, we have
raised the question whether other writers also make
this combination. The divine self-predication occurs
many times by itself, apart from the covenant formula,
and the covenant formula occurs a number of times apart
from the self-predication. It is significant that four
Old Testament sources connect the two -- the P document,
the Holiness Code, Jeremiah, and Ezekiel. These sources
are all concerned with interpreting the meaning of the
fall of Jerusalem and the exile in Babylon. As they
look forward to the future, these sources all anticipate
a new covenant relationship that will have its basis in
divine grace and will entail covenant obligation on the
part of the people. As one way of expressing this
expectation, these sources use "I am Yahweh" in close
conjunction with the covenant formula. The fact that
II Isaiah also links the divine self-predication with

the covenant formula indicates that he too anticipates
a new covenant relationship that will be made possible
by Yahweh's redemptive grace and will include covenant
obedience on the part of the people. For II Isaiah the
covenant formula -- like the expression "I am Yahweh"
itself -- embraces the themes of divine grace and human
responsibility, linking them so closely together that
the one necessarily entails the other.

6. Charge to Israel

        The self-predication "I am Yahweh" occurs also
in two passages that may be regarded as examples of the
"charge" to Israel or the "commissioning" of Israel to
fulfill a specific task. In this type of passage
Yahweh turns to Israel, addresses her directly, and
describes the task that he is appointing her to undertake. In the first passage, Is. 42:5-9, Yahweh gives
Israel a mission in relation to the nations of the
world: he appoints her to be "a covenant to the people,
a light to the nations" (Is. 42:6). In the second
passage, Is. 48:17-19, Yahweh charges Israel to remember
her ethical obligations as the people of God: he reminds
her of the importance of following his commandments,
with a poignant reference to her failure to do so in
pre-exilic times. The two passages are complementary
in the sense that the one refers to Israel's role on
the scene of world history and the other refers to her
internal life as the covenant people. In both passages,
the self-predication "I am Yahweh" introduces and
reinforces the statement of covenant obligation that
Israel is to accept.

        The first passage, Is. 42:5-9, opens with a
reference to Yahweh as the Creator of the heavens and

the earth (Is. 42:5). As frequently in II Isaiah, this reference to Yahweh as Creator supports the belief that Yahweh is powerful and able to intervene in human history. In this passage, in particular, the reference to Yahweh as Creator of the entire earth helps prepare the way for the affirmation that he will work through Israel in a way that will affect the other nations of the earth (Is. 42:6-7). The self-predication "I am Yahweh" in vs. 6 introduces the specific word that Yahweh addresses to Israel -- his charge to her to be "a covenant to the people, a light to the nations" (vs. 6). Israel's task is defined more specifically in vs. 7 in terms of healing the blindness of those who can not see and giving freedom to those in captivity. These references to blindness and captivity are probably figurative ways, as John McKenzie suggests, of depicting the ignorance of Yahweh and the service of false gods.[76] As "a covenant to the people," therefore, Israel is to mediate between Yahweh and the peoples of the world, bringing these peoples a true knowledge of Yahweh and giving them the opportunity to receive his salvation (cf. Is. 49:6). The repetition of "I am Yahweh" in Is. 42:8 echoes the use of this expression in vs. 6 and brings to a close this specific charge to Israel as she receives the definition of her role on the scene of world history.

　　　　This interpretation of Is. 42:5-9 as Yahweh's "charge" to Israel assumes that the passage is indeed addressed to the people of Israel (or in particular to the exiles in Babylon, who at this juncture receive the special task of representing what Israel is to be and to do). In a similar way, this interpretation assumes that the passage was written by II Isaiah himself rather than a later author or redactor. In developing

any interpretation of Is. 42:5-9, we must be aware of
several issues -- this passage seems to be closely
related to the preceding Servant Song in Is. 42:1-4;
the four Servant Songs (Is. 42:1-4; 49:1-6; 50:4-9;
52:13-53:12) may or may not form a distinct stratum in
the writings of II Isaiah, and they may or may not come
from II Isaiah himself; the "servant" in these Servant
Songs may or may not be Israel. Modern scholarship
reflects different views concerning these issues.
Westermann, for example, believes that the first three
Servant Songs were written by II Isaiah himself, but
inserted into his writings at some later time, and that
the passage Is. 42:5-8(9) is a later development of the
first Servant Song, although it has its basis in an
oracle of II Isaiah himself.[77] McKenzie believes that
the four Servant Songs were probably written by a
disciple of II Isaiah, and then still later an editor
wrote the "responses" that follow the first three songs
(Is. 42:5-9; 49:7-13; 50:10-11), relating the "servant"
to II Isaiah himself or assuming that the author of the
Servant Songs had intended this reference.[78]
Muilenburg, in contrast, emphasizes the similarities
between the Servant Songs and the remainder of II
Isaiah. On the basis of parallels in vocabulary and
motifs, as well as the argument that the first three
songs are integral parts of larger literary units, he
concludes that II Isaiah himself wrote the Servant Songs
and that the servant is to be identified as Israel.[79]

        In terms of vocabulary and ideas, Is. 42:5-9 is
probably related most closely to Is. 49:1-13 -- i.e.,
the second Servant Song and its sequel. Is. 42:6, for
example, has close parallels in Is. 49:1, 6, 8; Is.
42:7 has parallels in Is. 49:9; and Is. 42:8 finds an
echo in Is. 49:3. The ideas are common to both passages

that Yahweh has called, has kept, has given as a
covenant to the people and a light to the nations, to
help the prisoners and those in darkness, for the sake
of his glory. Thus Is. 42:5-9 would seem to be
addressed to the same person or group as Is. 49:1-13.
At the same time, it is also important to notice that
Is. 42:5-9 has parallels in II Isaiah apart from the
Servant Songs. The description of Yahweh as Creator of
the earth often functions in II Isaiah to support and
introduce the affirmation that he is acting in history
in a way that affects Israel (Is. 42:5; cf. 40:27-31;
44:24-28; 45:18-19; 50:1-3; 51:9-11, 12-16). In a
similar way, the idea that Yahweh "calls" is applied
elsewhere to the people of Israel (Is. 42:6; cf. 41:9;
43:1; 48:12; 54:6), and the idea that he "takes by the
hand" has parallels in a salvation oracle, addressed to
Israel (Is. 42:6; cf. 41:9, 13). The thought that
Yahweh will not share his "glory" or his "praise" seems
to find a complement elsewhere in the assertions that
Yahweh will be glorified in Israel, and Israel is to
declare the praise of Yahweh (Is. 42:8; cf. 44:23 and
43:21).

These parallels indicate that the terminology
and ideas of Is. 42:5-9 are closely related, not only
to Is. 49:1-13, but also to other passages in II Isaiah
which clearly refer to Yahweh's activities in relation
to Israel. The parallels with these other passages
also suggest, in turn, that Is. 49:1-13 itself describes
the task that Yahweh assigns to Israel. This would
support the view that the "servant" of the Servant Songs
is Israel, just as the servant outside the Servant Songs
is clearly Israel (e.g., Is. 41:8-9; 44:1-2, 21; 45:4;
48:20). In any event, these data would all suggest
that it is appropriate to describe Is. 42:5-9 as a

"charge to Israel," in which Yahweh commissions Israel
to be "a covenant to the people, a light to the nations"
(Is. 42:6). Is. 42:5-9 does indeed appear to be closely
related to the preceding passage, Is. 42:1-4, but it
functions more as a continuation or development than as
a "response" to the earlier passage. In Is. 42:1-4,
Yahweh introduces and presents the Servant, or Israel
in her role as servant; in Is. 42:5-9, Yahweh turns to
Israel, addresses her directly, and bestows on her the
commission that she is to undertake.

The relationship between these two passages --
Is. 42:1-4 and 42:5-9 -- helps to clarify the connection
between the commission that Israel receives and the
covenant that she has had with Yahweh throughout her
history. Israel can become "a covenant to the people"
only because she herself already stands in a covenant
relationship to Yahweh. The fact that Israel can
mediate a covenant between Yahweh and the peoples of
the world must presuppose the existence of a covenant
between Yahweh and Israel. The nature of the covenant
to be made "through" Israel, in turn, reflects the
content of the existing covenant "with" Israel. In
relation to the countries of the world, Israel is to
establish "justice" (mishpat) and bring Yahweh's "law"
(torah). She can be commissioned to do this because
her own covenant with Yahweh includes justice and law.
In this way II Isaiah wishes to indicate that Israel
will continue to value and preserve the sense of
covenant obligation that she derives from the Sinai
covenant. At the same time, she will help the peoples
of the world understand that knowledge of Yahweh as the
one true God (Is. 42:8) entails acceptance of the
responsibilities of covenant obligation (Is. 42:4).
Muilenburg's comment on Is. 42:4 is especially

suggestive in this regard because it calls attention to
the continuing influence of the Sinai covenant in the
commission that Israel receives: "Covenant (b^erîth) and
teaching (tôrāh) belong together; the covenant people
have been entrusted with teaching or law (cf. Exod.
19-24; etc.)."[80]

    We should also notice that the poem in Is. 51:
1-8 is closely related to Is. 42:1-9 and 49:1-13. It
helps to explain these other passages, and in turn it
is illumined by them. Each stanza begins with an
imperative, "hearken" or "listen," addressed to Israel
(Is. 51:1, 4, 7). Each stanza also highlights the term
tsedeq, which probably has a soteriological meaning
("deliverance") rather than an ethical meaning
("righteousness") throughout the poem (Is. 51:1, 5, 7;
the synonym tsedaqah also occurs in vss. 6, 8). The
structure of the poem follows a logical progression of
thought. In the first stanza, Yahweh promises Israel
that he will deliver her from exile, just as he originally called and guided Abraham and Sarah (Is. 51:1-3).
In the second stanza, Yahweh again addresses Israel
("my people") but describes the plans that he has for
the other nations of the world ("the peoples," "the
coastlands"; Is. 51:4-6). He will bring "deliverance"
(tsedeq) and "salvation" (yesha'), and he will send
"law" (torah) and "justice" (mishpat). Theologically,
the first two words express the grace that Yahweh offers
to the peoples of the world, while the last two words
represent the theme of covenant obligation as an
expression of the appropriate response that the nations
are to make to Yahweh's grace. The fact that Yahweh is
addressing Israel but referring to the other peoples of
the world implies that Israel must have a role in
communicating Yahweh's deliverance and salvation, law

and justice. Yahweh, therefore, can say that his
justice will go forth "for a light to the peoples"
because Israel herself is called to be "a covenant to
the people, a light to the nations" (Is. 42:6; cf. 49:
6, 8). In the third stanza of the poem, Yahweh reassures Israel that she can "fear not" because of the
promise that he has made to her in the first stanza and
the role that he has depicted for her in the second
stanza (Is. 51:7-8). The themes of grace and covenant
obligation reappear at the beginning of this stanza:
Israel is the people who know "deliverance" and have
"law" in their heart (Is. 51:7). Because Israel herself
is acquainted with grace and covenant obligation (Is.
51:7-8), she can serve as Yahweh's instrument in communicating these realities to the peoples of the world
(Is. 51:4-6). As in Is. 42:1-9, it is evident in Is.
51:4-8 that the covenant "through" Israel is a reflection of the covenant "with" Israel.

We may turn now to the second passage in which
the self-predication "I am Yahweh" occurs in a "charge"
to Israel that defines some important aspect of her
role as the covenant people. In this passage (Is. 48:
17-19) the divine self-predication functions especially
to introduce and reinforce the solemn reminder that
Israel is always expected to fulfill her covenant
obligations as the people of Yahweh: "I am Yahweh your
God, who teaches you to profit, who leads you in the way
you should go" (Is. 48:17). The verse employs the
participial style, in which "who teaches" and "who
leads" are literally "teaching" and "leading." The
participles indicate that Yahweh's activity of teaching
and leading his people is "continual" and "uninterrupted."[81] In the specific historical situation of II
Isaiah, these participles emphasize that Yahweh still

continues his activities of providing instruction and
guidance during the time of Israel's exile in Babylon;
the participles suggest, further, that Yahweh's
activities during the exile are an "uninterrupted"
continuation of his activities during the pre-exilic
period and at the same time an anticipation of the
teaching and guidance that he will provide for the
exiles after their return to their homeland. Yahweh,
therefore, still calls Israel to fulfill her covenant
obligations, just as he called her in the past and will
continue to call her in the future.

The verb translated "profit" (ya'al) seems to
have the meaning of benefitting or accomplishing something worthwhile. In other passages, for example, II
Isaiah asserts that idols of foreign gods do not profit
(Is. 44:9-10) and Babylon herself does not succeed or
profit (Is. 47:12). In a similar way, Jeremiah argued
that other gods, deceitful words, and false prophets
all fail to "profit" or have some effect that would be
of benefit to people (Jer. 2:8, 11; 7:8; 23:32). When
II Isaiah writes that Yahweh teaches Israel to "profit,"
he apparently means primarily that Yahweh expects
Israel to follow his commandments so that she can
receive the appropriate rewards for her obedience (cf.
Is. 48:18-19). At the same time, the word "profit" may
well suggest that Israel is to "accomplish something
worthwhile" by fulfilling her role on the scene of
world history. Internally, Israel is to "profit" by
obeying the commandments of the type represented by the
Sinai covenant. Externally, she may also "profit" by
fulfilling her commission of communicating the knowledge
of Yahweh to the other peoples of the world.

The formula of divine self-predication in Is.
48:17 is associated most immediately with the theme of

covenant obligation: "I am Yahweh your God, who teaches
you . . . who leads you . . ." We should also notice,
however, that the whole passage opens with a clear
affirmation of divine grace: "Thus says Yahweh, your
Redeemer . . ." As Redeemer (goel), Yahweh takes the
part of Israel, vindicates her rights, and promotes her
welfare. Rather than treating her strictly as she
deserves, he acts out of grace, on the basis of his
love for her (cf. Is. 43:4). This affirmation of
Yahweh's grace continues to govern the entire passage,
Is. 48:17-19. In this respect the self-predication "I
am Yahweh" in Is. 48:17 is closely associated with the
theme of grace as well as the theme of covenant
obligation or law.

7. Address to Cyrus

We may turn now to Is. 45:1-8, a passage that
may be described as Yahweh's "address to Cyrus" or his
"commissioning of Cyrus." In this passage Yahweh
speaks directly to Cyrus, designated as his "messiah"
or "anointed one," i.e., the one whom he has commissioned to fulfill a specific task (Is. 45:1). Cyrus
has already been introduced as the "shepherd" of Yahweh
who was to fulfill Yahweh's purpose (Is. 44:28). The
present passage, describing Cyrus as the "anointed one,"
reiterates the thought that Yahweh has chosen Cyrus for
a specific task, and then it goes on to describe this
task in greater detail.
This is the only passage in which II Isaiah
represents Yahweh as speaking directly to Cyrus. Other
passages refer to Cyrus only in the third person, as
"one from the east whom victory meets at every step"
(Is. 41:2) or "a bird of prey from the east" (Is. 46:11;

cf. 41:25; 44:28; 45:13; 48:14-15). Since II Isaiah
thinks of Yahweh as the universal God, the Creator of
all the earth and the Lord of all history, it is logical
that he would depict Yahweh as addressing Cyrus directly
and commissioning him to undertake a specific task. If
II Isaiah was familiar with the Cyrus Cylinder, in which
Cyrus attributed his success to the god Marduk, then
perhaps he was developing a polemical argument at this
point asserting that Yahweh, rather than Marduk, was
guiding the victorious career of Cyrus. At the same
time it is important to recognize that II Isaiah is
also thinking of Israel as the audience to which this
passage is directed. Yahweh is speaking to Cyrus, but
he speaks for the benefit of Israel, and Israel hears
or reads the passage in its spoken or written form.
Yahweh's words to Cyrus are also his words to Israel:
his promises of help to Cyrus are also promises to
Israel, and his commissioning of Cyrus becomes part of
his charge to Israel.

The other allusions that II Isaiah makes to
Cyrus also illustrate this close relationship between
Yahweh's plans for Cyrus and his plans for Israel.
Although it is very uncertain how the writings of II
Isaiah originated -- whether they were, for example, a
unified composition from the beginning or whether they
represent a collection of relatively short, self-
contained utterances -- it is suggestive, at least,
that in the present form of the writings a reference to
Cyrus is always followed by a reference to Israel. The
trial scene of Is. 41:1-4, for example, includes a
reference to Cyrus as part of the testimony that
supports Yahweh's claim to be the sole God who is
sovereign over the course of history: "Who stirred up
one from the east whom victory meets at every step?"

(Is. 41:2). The fact that Yahweh is guiding the
successful career of Cyrus provides evidence that he
alone can work effectively in history. This trial
scene is followed by a short passage that depicts the
effect of the trial on the other peoples of the world
(Is. 41:5-7), and this is followed in turn by a longer
passage that describes the results of the trial as they
affect Israel (Is. 41:8-16). This passage consists of
two salvation oracles in which Yahweh assures Israel
that he has made the decision now to deliver her from
exile. Yahweh, therefore, guides the career of Cyrus
as a way of realizing his plans for his people Israel.
In a similar way, the reference to Cyrus within a trial
scene (Is. 41:21-29) is followed closely by a reference
to Israel's role as servant of Yahweh (Is. 42:1-9).
Other references to Cyrus occur within a hymn of self-
praise (Is. 44:24-28) and in disputations with Israel
(Is. 45:9-13; 46:8-13); these passages also incorporate
references to Yahweh's plans on behalf of Israel. The
same structure of thought is evident in chapter 48, in
which an announcement of salvation (Is. 48:12-16)
precedes the statement of Yahweh's charge to Israel
(Is. 48:17-19). Wherever II Isaiah alludes to Yahweh's
plans for Cyrus, he also goes on to speak of Yahweh's
plans for Israel.

This pattern of thought helps us understand the
function of the self-predication "I am Yahweh" as it
occurs in Yahweh's address to Cyrus in Is. 45:1-8. It
is directed most specifically to Cyrus, of course, but
it is directed to Israel in the sense that Israel also
hears the passage and understands it as a statement of
Yahweh's intentions for her. II Isaiah encourages
Israel to understand the passage in this way by indicating that Yahweh calls Cyrus for the sake of Israel:

"For the sake of my servant Jacob, and Israel my chosen,
I call you by your name . . ." (Is. 45:4). This address
to Cyrus is distinctive, not only because it is the only
passage in which Yahweh speaks directly to Cyrus, but
also because it employs the expression "I am Yahweh" so
frequently (four times, in Is. 45:3, 5, 6, 7). All
these occurrences of the formula are addressed to Israel
as well as to Cyrus.

The address to Cyrus opens with an introduction
that identifies the speaker and the person addressed:
"Thus says Yahweh to his anointed, to Cyrus" (Is. 41:1).
The remainder of the verse indicates that Yahweh has
already begun to help Cyrus in his successful career of
conquest. In this way the introduction leads into the
next main section (vss. 2-4), in which Yahweh addresses
Cyrus and gives a poetic description of the help that
he will provide: "I will go before you and level the
mountains . . ." (Is. 41:2). At the close of this
section Yahweh explains the immediate purpose and the
further goal of his actions. His immediate purpose is
"that you [Cyrus] may know that I am Yahweh, the God of
Israel, who call you by your name" (Is. 41:3). His
further goal is that he is acting "for the sake of my
servant Jacob, and Israel my chosen" (Is. 45:4). The
formula of divine self-predication, therefore, conveys
Yahweh's intention that Cyrus will come to know him;
Yahweh's realization of this intention, at the same
time, points beyond itself to become a way in which he
will help his people Israel.

The next main section of the passage, vss. 5-7,
continues the direct address to Cyrus and also exhibits
some of the stylistic features of the hymn of self-
praise. At the beginning of vs. 5 and again at the end
of vs. 6, Yahweh speaks in terms of the formula of

exclusiveness: "I am Yahweh, and there is no other."
Between these two occurrences of the formula Yahweh
indicates that his purpose is universal in scope; he is
helping Cyrus "that men may know, from the rising of
the sun and from the west, that there is none besides
me" (Is. 45:6). At the end of vs. 7, after a succinct
summary of his activity in the spheres of nature and
history, Yahweh describes himself in terms that echo
the formula of incomparability: "I am Yahweh, who do
all these things." The implication here is that no one
else can do all these things, and no one else, therefore,
is like Yahweh. The whole verse ends with a poetic
description of the new era of salvation that is at hand:
deliverance (tsedeq) will come down from the heavens,
and salvation (yesha') and deliverance (tsedaqah) will
spring forth from the earth (Is. 45:8). This closing
verse corresponds to the first verse of the passage; it
forms an inclusion with the opening verse by depicting
the final outcome of Yahweh's initial decision to
"commission" or "anoint" Cyrus to fulfill his purpose.

Although this passage has the literary form of
an address to Cyrus, we have also seen that II Isaiah
presents it as part of his message to Israel. In this
respect it is important to ask what the passage means
to Israel; in particular, we may ask how the examples
of the self-predication "I am Yahweh" function as part
of the prophet's message to Israel. When we examine
the passage in this light, we find that the examples of
self-predication are closely associated with the themes
of grace and covenant responsibility. On the one hand,
they express the grace that Yahweh bestows on Israel.
On the other hand, they point to the task that Israel
receives in fulfilling her role as the covenant people
of Yahweh.

II Isaiah undoubtedly intends that Israel, as
well as Cyrus, should understand the meaning of the
self-predication "I am Yahweh, the God of Israel, who
call you by your name" (Is. 45:3). Israel is to perceive that Yahweh calls Cyrus and works through him for
her own benefit, as the prophet indicates in vs. 4:
"For the sake of my servant Jacob, and Israel my chosen,
I call you by your name." In this sense the divine
self-predication in vs. 3, addressed formally to Cyrus,
communicates Yahweh's grace to his people Israel.
Yahweh is guiding the successful career of Cyrus because
Cyrus, in turn, will set the exiles free and help them
return to their homeland.

In a similar way the next two examples of the
self-predication also express Yahweh's grace to Israel.
The formula of exclusiveness, "I am Yahweh, and there
is no other," occurs at the beginning of Is. 45:5 and
at the end of vs. 6. These two examples communicate
the sense of Yahweh's grace by reassuring Israel that
her God alone is truly God; she can look to him for
deliverance, in the sure knowledge that the gods of
other peoples can pose no hindrance to his work. At
the same time, these two examples of the self-predication
have the function of presenting the universal scope of
Yahweh's purpose: "that men may know, from the rising
of the sun and from the west, that there is none besides
me" (vs. 6). When Israel hears these words, she is
reminded that she shares in the task of helping the
world perceive that Yahweh alone is God. She is to be
a witness on behalf of Yahweh, appearing in the "world
court" and testifying to his deeds (Is. 43:8-13), and
as the servant of Yahweh she is to be "a covenant to
the people, a light to the nations" (Is. 42:6). At this
point, therefore, Israel is reminded that Yahweh's deeds

through Cyrus are not only expressions of his grace to
her, but also measures that will help her fulfill her
own role on the scene of world history.

The final example of the self-predication in this
passage also expresses the themes of grace and covenant
obligation as they affect Israel. Yahweh describes his
creative powers in the spheres of nature and history:
he makes "light" and "darkness," he produces "weal" and
"woe." His self-predication then summarizes his role
as Lord of nature and history: "I am Yahweh, who do all
these things" (Is. 45:7). As Israel hears these words,
she is assured that Yahweh can indeed show his grace to
her by delivering her from captivity. Yet the passage
continues with a poetic description of the "deliverance"
and "salvation" that Yahweh will send to the earth.
Since these terms are worldwide in scope, they must
refer to Yahweh's intentions toward the whole world as
well as his plans for Israel herself (cf. Is. 45:22-23;
51:4-8). Israel, therefore, is reminded once again of
her responsibility to make Yahweh's salvation known
throughout the world. She understands these words in
the light of Yahweh's direct commission to her, "I will
give you as a light to the nations, that my salvation
may reach to the end of the earth" (Is. 49:6).

B. "I am God"

We may turn now to another form of divine self-
predication, "I am God," which II Isaiah uses occasionally throughout his writings. This expression has the
form ani eloheka ("I am your God") in Is. 41:10, ani el
in Is. 43:12; 45:22, and anoki el in Is. 46:9. It is
very uncertain whether II Isaiah intended any difference
in meaning between the two words for "God" (elohim, el)

or the two words for "I" (ani, anoki). It is possible
that el is even more general or neutral in reference
than elohim; it would be consistent with such a
difference that II Isaiah uses el in addressing the
Gentile nations of the world (Is. 45:22) and elohim in
addressing Israel (Is. 41:10). Yet he also uses el
when Yahweh is speaking to Israel herself (Is. 43:12;
46:9). Whether or not II Isaiah wished to distinguish
between el and elohim, it is clear that these two words
for "God" are general terms which need to acquire a
specific reference through their use in a particular
context. In this respect they differ from the term
Yahweh, the proper name of the God of Israel.

   In section III.B., when we examined the use of
the expression "I am God," we saw that it occurs only
ten times in Old Testament writings apart from II
Isaiah. The general meaning of the words for "God"
would explain why Old Testament tradition used "I am
God" so seldom, especially in contrast to the frequent
use of the more specific self-predication "I am Yahweh."
At the same time, it is rather unexpected that II Isaiah
actually uses "I am God" four times, since the remainder
of the entire Old Testament uses it only ten times.
The fact that II Isaiah thinks so vividly of Yahweh as
God over the entire world, together with the fact that
he so often addresses the Gentile nations or at least
has them in mind, may well account for his relatively
frequent use of the expression "I am God." This form of
divine self-predication becomes, for II Isaiah, an
especially vivid way to express the conviction that
Yahweh is the sole, universal God who is sovereign over
all the peoples of the world.

   In section III.B. we also saw that the self-
predication "I am God," as a formula within Old

Testament tradition, evidently originated in theophanies to individual persons during the patriarchal
period. Later it was preserved in the context of the
worship of the Jerusalem temple. Usually the formula
expressed the theme of grace -- i.e., God's promise of
some form of help or blessing. The formula expressed
the theme of law only once, in Ps. 50:7, where it
occurred within a liturgical counterpart to the covenant
lawsuit. When we analyze the use of the formula in II
Isaiah, we will be especially interested in asking to
what extent it expresses the theme of law as well as
that of grace. If II Isaiah associates the formula
prominently with "law" as well as "grace," he will be
giving an emphasis to the idea of law or covenant
obligation that the formula did not convey in previous
Old Testament usage.

1. Trial Scene: Yahweh and the Nations

This question concerning the connotations of the
formula "I am God" arises in the trial scene depicted
in Is. 43:8-13. As we saw above, in section IV.A.1.,
this is the type of trial scene in which Yahweh summons
the nations of the world to appear in court, and then
he demonstrates that he, rather than other gods, is
truly sovereign over the course of history. The trial
scene involves the other peoples of the world, yet at
the same time it is addressed to the exiles in Babylon
as a way of reassuring them that Yahweh can indeed
deliver them. Within the trial scene, furthermore,
Yahweh addresses the exiles directly, calling upon them
to serve as witnesses on his behalf and testify to his
deeds:

"You are my witnesses," says Yahweh,
"and my servant whom I have chosen,
that you may know and believe me
and understand that I am He."
(Is. 43:10)

This is the setting in which II Isaiah uses all
three forms of self-predication: "I, I am Yahweh" (Is.
43:11), "I am He" (vss. 10, 13), and "I am God" (vs. 13).
Within this setting the prophet also expresses several
distinct ideas. These include the designation of Israel
as "witnesses" and "servant," not only that Israel may
testify on behalf of Yahweh, but also that Israel herself may increase in understanding and faith (vs. 10);
the idea of the exclusiveness or uniqueness of Yahweh
("before me no god was formed, nor shall there be any
after me," vs. 10); and the idea of the incomparability
of Yahweh ("I am God . . . there is none who can deliver
from my hand; I work and who can hinder it?" vs. 13).

Although the structure of the whole passage
requires that a certain form of self-predication stand
in close proximity to a particular idea, it would be
artificial to overemphasize this kind of connection.
The significance of the passage as a whole makes it
much more likely that the three forms of self-predication
all function to express and reinforce the ideas that the
trial scene presents. In vs. 13, therefore, the formula
"I am God" does not refer merely to the theme of incomparability; it also refers to the exclusiveness of
Yahweh and to the role of Israel as "witnesses" and
"servant." In this way the self-predication "I am God"
expresses the themes of both grace and law. It presents
Yahweh as the unique and incomparable God who works in
history to help his people, and it reminds Israel that
her role as the covenant people involves giving testimony

on behalf of Yahweh and growing in her own knowledge,
understanding, and faith (vs. 10).

2. Salvation Oracle

As we noted earlier, in section IV.A.2., the
salvation oracles have the function of reassuring Israel
that Yahweh has determined to help her by delivering
her from exile. In these oracles Yahweh speaks to
Israel, identifies himself, assures her of his presence
with her, announces the decision that he has made to
help her, and depicts the consequences of this decision.
It is consistent with the personal tone of direct
address that the self-predication in the oracle in Is.
41:8-13 has the possessive suffix: "fear not, for I am
with you, be not dismayed, for I am your God" (Is. 41:
10). II Isaiah evidently felt that the simple self-
predication "I am God" (ani elohim) would have been too
vague or neutral within the setting of a salvation
oracle. In addition, he uses the term elohim occasionally to denote the gods of other nations (e.g., Is. 41:
23; 42:17). For these reasons he evidently thought it
more suitable here to use the possessive form, "I am
your God" (ani eloheka), as a way of emphasizing the
relationship between God and Israel that finds special
expression in the salvation oracle.

In this particular passage the divine self-
predication, "I am your God," appears to be associated
only with the theme of grace, rather than grace and
law together. The salvation oracle, by its very nature,
refers to the gracious deliverance or "salvation" that
Yahweh freely offers his people, and it would seem that
this type of passage could not accommodate any corres-
ponding reference to the covenant obligation of the

people. This is the case in all five examples of the
salvation oracle in II Isaiah (Is. 41:8-13, 14-16; 43:
1-3, 4-7; 44:1-5); all of these express the theme of
God's grace without any reference to law or covenant
obligation. We must look to other forms of speech,
therefore, to find examples of divine self-predication
that remind the people of law as well as grace.

3. Disputation with Israel

We meet a somewhat similar situation when we
analyze the self-predication "I am God" in Is. 46:9,
which occurs within a disputation with Israel (Is. 46:
8-13). In this passage Yahweh seeks to overcome the
exiles' mood of resignation and self-pity by assuring
them that he is indeed about to take action on their
behalf. He reminds the exiles that he has announced
his intentions beforehand (vs. 10), that he is calling
Cyrus, the "bird of prey from the east" (vs. 11), that
he is bringing near his "deliverance" and his
"salvation" (tsedaqah and teshu'ah, vs. 12). The self-
predication, standing near the beginning of the passage,
reads literally, "I am God (anoki el), and there is no
other; God (elohim), and there is none like me" (vs. 9).
The self-predication illustrates how II Isaiah
can use el and elohim synonymously. It also expresses
the themes of exclusiveness ("there is no other") and
incomparability ("there is none like me"). These themes
are more characteristic of the hymn of self-praise; but
as we saw earlier, in section IV.A.5., the disputation
has a tendency to attract elements from other types of
speech. In this setting the themes of exclusiveness
and incomparability reinforce the message that Yahweh
is indeed able to deliver Israel from exile. They also

help to make it clear that the general terms el and
elohim can refer here to none other than Yahweh.

Like the salvation oracle, the disputation as a
specific form of speech has the general purpose of reassuring the exiles that Yahweh is indeed going to
deliver them. In this respect it is not surprising
that the formula "I am God" in Is. 46:9 is associated
primarily with the theme of grace -- i.e., as the
unique and incomparable God, Yahweh has announced his
intentions beforehand and is now working through Cyrus
to bring deliverance and salvation to his people. The
particular question that we must ask is whether the
divine self-predication in this passage is also
associated in any way with the theme of law or covenant
obligation. Here it is important to notice that the
exiles are addressed as "you transgressors" (vs. 8) and
"you stubborn of heart, you who are far from deliverance" (vs. 12). To the extent that these expressions
may refer to the people's failure to fulfill their
covenant obligations, then the self-predication "I am
God" would serve to express the theme of law as well as
grace.

The description of the exiles as "stubborn of
heart" and "far from deliverance" probably means that
they persist in their mood of self-pity and refuse to
believe that Yahweh is about to intervene on their
behalf. These terms, that is, probably refer to the
exiles' attitude toward their situation rather than to
any failure to meet covenant obligations. The designation of the exiles as "transgressors," on the other
hand, can well refer to their obligations as members of
the covenant people. Directly, the term must refer to
the whole period before the year 587 B.C., during which
the people of Israel failed to fulfill their covenant

responsibilities and so eventually suffered the loss of
their country. II Isaiah is referring primarily to
this time, just as he refers to it in Is. 42:24-25 and
43:26-28. He regards the exiles as "transgressors" in
the sense that they stand in continuity with the pre-
exilic Israel that persistently failed to meet covenant
obligations and eventually had to suffer the consequence.
At the same time, II Isaiah is indicating in an indirect
manner that the exiles must still acknowledge and
fulfill their sense of covenant responsibility. They
still belong to a covenant people that must meet
religious and ethical obligations in maintaining their
relationship with their God, and they must anticipate a
future that will involve the continuation of this sense
of covenant responsibility as their faithful response
to new manifestations of divine grace. In this very
important way, therefore, the self-predication "I am
God" in Is. 46:9 serves to remind the exiles of the
theme of "law" as well as "grace."

4. Address to the Nations

Just as the disputation in Is. 46:8-13 refers
indirectly to Israel's continuing responsibility as a
covenant people, so the "address to the nations" in Is.
45:22-23 serves to remind Israel herself of her role on
the scene of world history. In this passage Yahweh
turns to the nations of the world and proclaims his
intention to include them within the scope of the
salvation that he offers:

> Turn to me and be saved,
>   all the ends of the earth!
> For I am God (ani el),
>   and there is no other.

> By myself I have sworn,
> > from my mouth has gone forth
> > > in righteousness
> > a word that shall not return:
> > "To me every knee shall bow,
> > every tongue shall swear."
> > > > (Is. 45:22-23)

This passage is especially significant because
it is the only one in which II Isaiah depicts Yahweh as
speaking directly to the nations of the world and
offering them salvation. Elsewhere Yahweh speaks to
the nations only in the context of trial scenes, in
which his purpose is to demonstrate that he alone is
God (Is. 41:1; 45:20-21; cf. 41:21-24; 43:8-9). In
another group of passages, in which Yahweh does allude
to the salvation of the nations, he is speaking to
other audiences (i.e., Israel or Cyrus; cf. Is. 42:6-7;
45:6-8; 49:6; 51:4-5). The present passage brings
together these stylistic and thematic motifs by
presenting Yahweh as speaking directly to the nations
and offering them salvation.

This address to the nations in Is. 45:22-23 is
closely related to the address to Cyrus earlier in the
chapter (Is. 45:1-8). As we saw above, in section
IV.A.7., the address to Cyrus is the only passage in
which II Isaiah represents Yahweh as speaking directly
to Cyrus; in this respect the address to Cyrus, the
Gentile, helps to prepare the way for the address to
the Gentile nations of the world. The address to Cyrus
also indicates that a major purpose of Yahweh's working
through Cyrus is that people throughout the world may
come to know that Yahweh alone is God (Is. 45:6). In
this respect too the address to Cyrus helps to prepare
the way for the address to the nations. Finally, in

the address to Cyrus, Yahweh is also speaking indirectly
to Israel, assuring her of salvation and reminding her
of her role in helping to make salvation known throughout the world. This indirect reference to Israel is
also implied in the address to the nations. As Israel
hears these words, she is reminded of her own role as
"a light to the nations" that Yahweh's salvation "may
reach to the end of the earth" (Is. 49:6). Israel,
indeed, can not hear these words that offer salvation
to the Gentiles without thinking of her own covenant
obligation in relation to the nations of the world.
Yahweh's address to the nations implies the calling of
Israel to fulfill her role on the scene of world events.

This survey indicates that II Isaiah uses the
self-predication "I am God" relatively often and with
an unexpected emphasis on the theme of covenant
obligation as well as divine grace. Whereas the
expression occurs only ten times in the other writings
of the Old Testament, II Isaiah uses it four times
within a relatively short series of chapters. Elsewhere in the Old Testament, the self-predication "I am
God" almost always expresses the theme of divine grace,
in the form of God's promise of help or blessing. The
four occurrences in II Isaiah also express the idea of
grace, but three of these occurrences also call
attention to Israel's role and responsibility as the
covenant people. The trial scene in Is. 43:8-13, for
example, presents Yahweh as the sole God who delivers
his people, but it also depicts Israel as the covenant
people who give testimony on behalf of Yahweh and grow
in knowledge, understanding, and faith. The salvation
oracle in Is. 41:8-13 conveys the motif of grace alone,
without at this point referring to the role of Israel
as the covenant people. The disputation in Is. 46:8-13,

however, uses the expression "I am God" to convey the
themes of both grace and law. Yahweh is working through
Cyrus to deliver his people, and the people are depicted
as "transgressors" in the sense that they stand in
continuity with the generations before 587 B.C. and are
still called to be a covenant community with ethical
obligations. In a similar way the address to the
nations in Is. 45:22-23 combines the themes of grace
and law. Yahweh's offer of salvation to the nations
presupposes salvation for Israel, since Israel must be
set free so that she can fulfill her role of making
known the salvation of Yahweh; this role in turn, is
also an expression of her covenant obligation as it is
defined now in relation to the nations of the world.

C. "I am He"

We may turn now to the third form of divine
self-predication, "I am He," which II Isaiah uses along
with "I am Yahweh" and "I am God." As we saw earlier,
in section III.C., this type of self-predication seems
to occur elsewhere in the Old Testament only in the
Song of Moses, in the form "I, even I, am He" (ani ani
hu, Deut. 32:39). The Song of Moses is an apologia on
behalf of Yahweh, presenting the argument that he is
"just and right" (Deut. 32:4) in treating his people as
he does. He must punish them for worshiping other gods,
but then he will also have mercy on them. To the extent
that the whole poem functions as a "witness" for Yahweh
against the people of Israel (Deut. 31:19), the poem
resembles the type of trial scene in which Yahweh
appears in the role of prosecutor, bringing charges
against Israel.

In its setting in the Song of Moses, the
expression "I, even I, am He" serves to express four
distinct motifs: the uniqueness of Yahweh as the sole
God, the role of Yahweh as sovereign over the course of
history, the grace of Yahweh in delivering his people
and showing mercy on them, and the law or covenant
obligation that Yahweh expects his people to fulfill.
When we analyze II Isaiah's use of "I am He," we may
ask whether he also uses the formula to express these
themes. As we noted above, the Song of Moses was most
probably written earlier than II Isaiah's own time,
although it is uncertain whether II Isaiah was acquainted with it. The Song of Moses does provide a possible
source, along with similar expressions in Jer. 14:22
and Ps. 102:27, from which II Isaiah could have learned
of the formula "I am He."

In contrast to the extreme rarity of "I am He"
elsewhere in the Old Testament, it is striking that II
Isaiah uses the expression eight times -- six times in
the form "I am He" (ani hu; Is. 41:4; 43:10, 13; 46:4;
48:12; 52:6), and twice in the form "I, I am He" (anoki
anoki hu; Is. 43:25; 51:12). This high frequency of
occurrence may well reflect an implicit polemic against
the "I style" of kings in the Ancient Near East. The
study by H.-M. Dion, referred to above (section IV.A.4.
and notes 67-68), suggested that II Isaiah was familiar
with the lavish praises that these monarchs addressed
to themselves at the beginning of votive inscriptions.
II Isaiah, in addition, may have been familiar with the
kind of claim that Nineveh had made for herself ("I am
and there is none else," Zeph. 2:15), and of course
II Isaiah himself refers to the similar claim advanced
by Babylon (Is. 47:8, 10). Against this background of
claims of the "I am" type, with their pretension to

unique power, status, and even divinity, II Isaiah
wishes to affirm unequivocally that Yahweh alone is
entitled to use this form of self-predication.

1. Trial Scene: Yahweh and the Nations

We may look first at II Isaiah's use of "I am He"
in the type of trial scene in which Yahweh summons the
nations of the world to appear with him in court and
determine who actually controls the course of history.
In section IV.A.1. above we analyzed this type of trial
scene, and we also looked at the two examples in which
II Isaiah uses the self-predication "I am He" (Is. 41:
1-4; 43:8-13). At this point we may note that in the
first example, Is. 41:1-4, "I am He" stands at the close
of the passage as a summary affirmation of the ideas
that the passage has expressed concerning Yahweh. These
include the sovereignty of Yahweh over the entire course
of history ("the first, and with the last," vs. 4), and
especially the activity of Yahweh in guiding the career
of Cyrus. Since Yahweh works through Cyrus to redeem
his people Israel, the expression "I am He" also conveys
the sense of Yahweh's grace to Israel. These themes all
find expression in the closing affirmation of the trial,
"I am Yahweh, the first, and with the last; I am He"
(vs. 4).

In the trial scene in Is. 43:8-13, the expression
"I am He" actually occurs twice, in verses 10 and 13,
along with the other forms of self-predication ("I, I am
Yahweh," vs. 11, and "I am God," vs. 13). This repetition and variety in the several forms of self-predication
highlight the importance of the passage. The formula
"I am He" stands at the close of major sections of the
trial -- the summons to witnesses (vs. 10) and the

statement of the verdict (vs. 13). In their context, these words help to express the themes of the uniqueness of Yahweh, his sovereignty over history, and his role as Savior in showing grace to Israel. The self-predication "I am He" also depicts Yahweh as the God who calls Israel to act in terms of her covenant obligation, fulfilling her role as "witnesses" and "servant," and growing at the same time in her own knowledge, faith, and understanding (vs. 10). In these ways the formula "I am He" calls attention to the close relationship between the themes of grace and law. It suggests that Yahweh's gift of grace can not be separated from his expectation that Israel will fulfill her covenant responsibilities; with reference to Israel herself, it suggests that Israel's acceptance of grace necessarily implies that she will also acknowledge her covenant obligation to Yahweh.

2. Announcement of Salvation

The self-predication "I am He" also occurs in another type of speech, the announcement of salvation, which we analyzed above in section IV.A.3. At that point we saw that II Isaiah used the formula "I am Yahweh" in connection with the themes of both grace and law in Is. 43:14-21, even though the announcement of salvation as a form of speech required that he emphasize the grace of the deliverance that Yahweh would soon provide for his people. In this section of our study we will be concerned with three other examples of the announcement of salvation -- Is. 46:1-4; 48:12-16; 52: 3-6. We may examine these with special regard for the question whether II Isaiah uses "I am He" to express the motif of covenant obligation as well as grace.

The first passage, Is. 46:1-4, presents a vivid picture of the statues of the two chief Babylonian gods, Bel and Nebo. Strapped on the backs of beasts of burden, the statues sway to and fro as they are carried along. It is uncertain whether II Isaiah is thinking here of a regular religious procession, such as the one that took place in the New Year's festival, or whether he is depicting in advance a last-minute attempt by the Babylonians to carry the statues of their gods to safety before their city falls. It is also uncertain exactly how this passage should be classified. It may suggest a satire, a taunt song, or a song of victory. It resembles a trial scene in the sense that Yahweh's role as Lord of history is contrasted with the inability of other gods to work effectively in history. It is included here under the rubric "announcement of salvation" because it comes to a climax in Yahweh's promise of deliverance to his people: "even to your old age I am He, and to gray hairs I will carry you. I have made, and I will bear; I will carry and will save" (vs. 4).

In other passages we have seen that the formula "I am He" expresses several distinct themes, such as the uniqueness of Yahweh, his sovereignty over the course of history, and his gracious action in delivering his people. The present passage would seem to express all of these themes. In contrasting Yahweh with gods that must be carried about on beasts of burden, the passage implies that Yahweh alone is truly God. In a similar way the passage presents Yahweh as Lord of history, in contrast to the Babylonian gods who can do nothing for their city. In an especially vivid contrast, the passage depicts Yahweh as the God who carries and saves his people, in comparison to Bel and Nebo, who must be carried on the backs of animals.

Since II Isaiah's main purpose in this passage
is to proclaim the salvation that Yahweh is bringing,
he makes no explicit mention of the covenant obligation
that Israel accepts in response to divine grace. It is
possible that II Isaiah refers to covenant obligation
indirectly when he compares Israel's history to the
span of a human life, from "birth" to "gray hairs"
(vss. 3-4). Through this comparison he suggests that
he is thinking of Yahweh, not simply as the God who
will soon bring deliverance from exile, but as the God
who supports and guides his people throughout the
entire course of their history. In this sense the
comparison would remind Israel of all the significant
events that she had experienced in her history,
including, for example, the covenant at Sinai as well
as the Exodus deliverance from bondage in Egypt. It is
only in this indirect, way, however, that II Isaiah
alludes here to the motif of covenant obligation or
law.

II Isaiah also uses the self-predication "I am
He" in another passage that may be classified tentatively as an announcement of salvation (Is. 48:12-16). The
passage begins with a summons to Israel, and then it
continues with the divine self-predication:

> Hearken to me, O Jacob,
>> and Israel, whom I called!
> I am He, I am the first,
>> and I am the last.
> My hand laid the foundation of the earth,
>> and my right hand spread out the
>> heavens;
> when I call to them,
>> they stand forth together.
>> (Is. 48:12-13)

It is significant that the formula "I am He" is associated here with Yahweh's role as sovereign over the entire course of history ("the first . . . the last") and then also with his role as Creator of the universe ("the earth . . . the heavens"). As so frequently in II Isaiah, the categories of "history" and "nature" are closely interrelated as spheres in which Yahweh's activity takes place. The idea that Yahweh "calls" or "speaks" helps to show the close interrelationship between these categories, and it also helps prepare the way for the following verses in this passage (vss. 14-16). Yahweh has "called" Israel (vs. 12), he "calls" the earth and the heavens into existence (vs. 13), he has "spoken and called" Cyrus of Persia to bring about the deliverance of his people Israel (vs. 15), and the course of events "from the beginning" has shown the continuity between Yahweh's word and its effect in reality (vs. 16). This emphasis on the reliable continuity between word and effect supports the statements concerning Yahweh's word that stand at important points in II Isaiah's writings: Yahweh's word concerning the deliverance of Israel "will stand for ever" (Is. 40:8); his word offering salvation to the nations of the earth "shall not return" (Is. 45:23); and his word that sums up his redemptive work "shall accomplish" that which he purposes (Is. 55:11).

Is. 48:12-16 may be classified tentatively as an announcement of salvation because its primary purpose is to proclaim to Israel that Yahweh is working through Cyrus for Israel's own benefit. The passage resembles a disputation in the sense that Yahweh seeks to remind Israel that he can and will intervene in history to help her. A disputation, however, would refer more directly to the mood of discouragement affecting the

exiles and the complaints that they express. The
passage resembles a trial scene in the sense that Yahweh
points to the successful career of Cyrus as evidence
that he alone can guide the course of history and he
alone, therefore, is truly God. In the actual trial
scenes, however, Yahweh summons the nations of the
world (or their gods) to appear in court and hear his
evidence. In the present passage Yahweh summons the
people of Israel to "assemble" and "draw near" to hear
his statement (Is. 48:14, 16). At this point the
message that he proclaims is addressed to Israel, even
though it closely resembles the evidence that he
presents elsewhere in trial scenes with the peoples of
the world.

In this passage the self-predication "I am He"
is closely associated with the ideas that Yahweh is
Lord of history, that he is Creator of the universe, and
that he is showing grace to Israel by delivering her
from exile. Verses 14-16, with their resemblance to
the trial scenes, also imply that Yahweh alone is truly
God. In itself, the passage does not connect the
formula "I am He" with the theme of law or covenant
obligation on the part of Israel. It does so only
indirectly and contextually, in the sense that this
passage (Is. 48:12-16) is followed by a charge to Israel
(Is. 48:17-19), in which Yahweh reminds Israel of the
continuing importance of following his commandments.
The two passages are complementary -- the first
announces the divine grace of deliverance, the second
depicts Israel's continuing covenant responsibility,
and both together lead up to the final instructions at
the close of the chapter, "Go forth from Babylon, flee
from Chaldea . . ." (Is. 48:20). This arrangement of
units, in which the announcement of salvation for Israel

is followed by the charge to Israel, may well derive
from II Isaiah himself.

A third passage which may be regarded as an
announcement of salvation is Is. 52:3-6. The passage
gives a brief, highly condensed survey of Israel's
history from the standpoint of her experiences of
suffering oppression. The main theme of the survey is
that the countries which oppressed Israel -- Egypt,
Assyria, and now Babylon -- never had any legitimate
claims upon her, so that Yahweh is fully justified now
in "redeeming" or taking back his people. The passage
culminates in a promise of deliverance in which the
self-predication "I am He" is prominent. Although the
style of this closing verse is awkward, a literal
translation will present the self-predication most
clearly: "Therefore my people shall know my name;
therefore in that day (they shall know) that I am He,
the one who speaks; here am I" (Is. 52:6).

The formula "I am He" in this passage expresses
the theme that Yahweh is the Lord of history who can
deliver his people from oppression. In particular, it
promises that Yahweh will show his grace to the exiles
by coming to save them. It is possible that "I am He"
may even convey the theme of renewed covenant obligation,
since the expectation that "my people shall know my
name" may well echo passages such as Ex. 3:13-14 and
20:1-2, in which knowing the name of Yahweh is an
intrinsic part of the complex of events by which the
people of Israel are introduced to Yahweh and enter
into covenant with him. In this respect the passage
would combine an announcement of salvation with a
promise of renewed covenant relationship, so that II
Isaiah would be bringing together once again the themes
of grace and law as complementary motifs within a
holistic understanding of Yahweh's nature and activity.

It is possible that this passage, Is. 52:3-6, is
a later addition to II Isaiah's writings. It seems to
be in prose, which is unusual in II Isaiah. The
reference to the oppression of Israel by Assyria and
the use of the expression "in that day" are not typical
of II Isaiah. From a stylistic point of view the
closing verse is especially awkward, so that the words
"they shall know" must be inserted to give a smooth
translation. On the other hand, the passage does fit
into its context. The first verse extends the thought
of the preceding verses (Is. 52:1-2), and the closing
verse introduces the following verses (Is. 52:7-10).
The idea that Yahweh will redeem his people (Is. 52:3)
echoes the thought of Is. 40:10, which depicts Yahweh
as the divine warrior who brings back his people as
spoils of war, and it also anticipates the similar
imagery in Is. 52:9-10. In spite of the difficulties
with the passage, therefore, it is very possible that
it may be regarded as genuine. For our present purposes
we may consider it tentatively as an authentic example
of II Isaiah's use of the formula "I am He."

3. Trial Scene: Yahweh and Israel

The expression "I am He" occurs also in Is. 43:
25-28, a passage which reflects a trial scene between
Yahweh and Israel. In the other trial scenes that we
have examined (sections IV.A.1., B.1., and C.1.),
Yahweh summons the nations of the world, or their gods,
inviting them to appear in court so that he can demonstrate that he alone is sovereign over the course of
history. In contrast, we are meeting now a type of
trial scene that involves Yahweh and Israel as the two
contending parties. In earlier tradition the prophet

Hosea had employed this form of speech, depicting
Yahweh as the plaintiff who was bringing a lawsuit (<u>rib</u>)
against Israel, the defendant (Hos. 4:1-3). In this
particular example Yahweh accuses Israel of not meeting
her obligations under the terms of the covenant: she
does not exhibit faithfulness, covenant loyalty, or
knowledge of God (vs. 1). More specifically, Yahweh
accuses Israel, in effect, of not observing the Ten
Commandments, since she is guilty of swearing, lying,
killing, stealing, and committing adultery (vs. 2).
Hosea does not actually state the verdict in this trial,
apparently because he regards Israel's guilt as self-
evident. Instead he gives a vivid portrayal of the
consequences of Israel's guilt, as they affect human
life and also the world of nature (vs. 3).

    The prophets Micah and Jeremiah also employed
this type of speech (Mic. 6:1-8; Jer. 2:4-13). Psalm
50, in addition, suggests that the perspective of this
type of trial was incorporated into the liturgical
praxis of the Jerusalem temple, so that the theophany
out of Zion signified the coming of Yahweh to judge his
people. Although these passages differ in detail,
somewhat like variations on a theme, they all rest on
the conditional nature of the Sinai covenant, as Yahweh
sought to make it clear at the beginning:"Now, therefore,
if you will obey my voice and keep my covenant, you
shall be my own possession among all peoples . . ." (Ex.
19:5). Yahweh is not obligated to maintain the covenant
relationship with Israel if she does not fulfill her
obligations. The terms of the covenant allow him to
bring Israel into court and charge her formally with
her failure to meet her religious and ethical responsibilities. Prophets such as Hosea and Micah warned that
Yahweh was legally entitled to repudiate the covenant

relationship with Israel. In the early sixth century
B.C., when Babylon was threatening the people of Israel,
Jeremiah announced that Yahweh was "weary of relenting"
(Jer. 15:6) and had finally decided to abrogate the
covenant.

In a similar way II Isaiah uses the imagery of
the law court to look back and explain the disastrous
events of 587 B.C.:

> I, I am He
>> who blots out your transgressions
>>> for my own sake,
>> and I will not remember your sins.
> Put me in remembrance, let us argue
>> together;
>> set forth your case, that you may
>>> be proved right.
> Your first father sinned,
>> and your mediators transgressed
>>> against me.
> Therefore I profaned the princes of
>> the sanctuary,
>> I delivered Jacob to utter destruction
>> and Israel to reviling.
>>> (Is. 43:25-28)

The second verse of this passage ("Put me in remembrance . . .") actually introduces the trial scene.
Yahweh summons Israel into court and charges her with
consistent failure to render obedience. Then on the
basis of this charge he explains why he was justified
in allowing Babylon to devastate the country in 587 B.C.
and take the people of Israel into exile. II Isaiah
stands in the tradition of the pre-exilic prophets in
concurring with this explanation and in utilizing the
trial scene as a vehicle for presenting it.

At first sight the opening verse of this passage
does not seem to belong to a trial scene. It presents
Yahweh as the one who forgives Israel rather than the
one who brings an indictment against her: "I, I am He
who blots out your transgressions for my own sake, and
I will not remember your sins" (Is. 43:25). In itself,
the verse reflects a basic theme in II Isaiah's outlook.
It extends the thought, expressed vividly at the very
beginning of II Isaiah's writings, that it is time now
for Israel to receive pardon and comfort because she
has suffered enough and more than enough for all her
sins (Is. 40:1-2). II Isaiah evidently places this
verse (Is. 43:25) in a proleptic position at the
beginning of the trial scene for two reasons: he wants
his fellow exiles to be assured that they are a forgiven
people, even though they sinned and were punished in
the past, and he also wants to prepare the way for the
salvation oracle that will immediately follow (Is. 44:
1-5) as a way of giving the exiles further assurance
that they are still called to be the servants of Yahweh
and they will soon be returning to their homeland. The
self-predication "I, I am He" and the salvation oracle
function as "brackets" around the trial scene and place
it within a context that relates more directly to II
Isaiah's own time. In their relationship to one another
the self-predication and the salvation oracle stand in
ascending parallelism, since the first speaks of divine
forgiveness and the second depicts the consequences of
this forgiveness.

With regard to our present study it is especially
important to notice, of course, that the formula "I, I
am He" serves primarily to express the theme of divine
forgiveness. This is closely related to the use of
"I am He" in settings that express Yahweh's grace in

delivering Israel in the original Exodus from Egypt or
in the coming restoration from captivity (Deut. 32:39;
Is. 41:4; 43:10, 13; 46:4; 48:12; 52:6). It is even
possible that the wording of "I, I am He" in Is. 43:25
(anoki anoki hu), with its repetition of "I" and its
use of the longer word for "I," was intentionally chosen
to produce a solemn, dignified tone that would be
especially suitable for communicating the theme of
divine forgiveness. There would seem to be no reason
to argue, on the other hand, that this solemn self-
predication expresses divine forgiveness in a way that
would cancel any sense of continuing covenant obligation
on the part of the people. The fact that II Isaiah uses
this formula at the beginning of a trial scene may
indicate that he is thinking holistically -- i.e., in
terms of the entire life-span of the people of Israel
as the covenant community, much as he is thinking of
Israel's lifetime from "birth" to "old age" in Is. 46:
1-4. In both passages he may well be alluding indirectly
to Israel's role as the covenant people of Yahweh, as
this role helps to define her identity throughout her
history.

4. Disputation with Israel

The last example of "I am He" that remains to be
examined in II Isaiah occurs in a disputation with
Israel, Is. 51:9-52:2. When we analyzed this passage
previously in section IV.A.5., we saw that it begins by
quoting the lament that the exiles in Babylon are raising
(Is. 51:9-10) and then continues with the reply that
Yahweh gives, in which he reassures the exiles that he
can and will deliver them from their distress (Is. 51:
12 ff.). Here it is especially important to note that

the formula of divine self-predication introduces this
response:

> I, I am He that comforts you;
>> who are you that you are afraid
>>> of man who dies,
>> of the son of man who is made
>>> like grass,
> and have forgotten Yahweh, your Maker,
>> who stretched out the heavens
>> and laid the foundations of the
>>> earth . . .?
>
>> (Is. 51:12-13)

As in the trial scene that we have just examined,
the self-predication here has the longer form, "I, I am
He" (anoki anoki hu). Here again, the prophet may have
chosen the longer form intentionally as an appropriate
way of communicating themes like divine forgiveness or
comfort. In the present passage, the statement that
Yahweh comforts continues with the closely related
thoughts that he protects, creates, delivers, and
sustains (vss. 12-14). The self-predication "I, I am
He" introduces all these themes and presents them as
sources of reassurance to the exiles who are lamenting
or complaining about their distress.

As we would expect in the response to a lament,
the divine self-predication in Is. 51:12 expresses the
motif of Yahweh's grace to his people. At the same
time we should notice that this self-predication leads
up to another ("For I am Yahweh your God . . ." vs. 15),
which in turn introduces a statement of the covenant
formula ("You are my people," vs. 16). When we analyzed
this passage earlier, we saw that the covenant formula
is a comprehensive idea that includes Yahweh's grace to
Israel and also Israel's covenant responsibility to

Yahweh. When II Isaiah introduces Yahweh's reply with the self-predication "I, I am He," he sets in motion a train of thought that emphasizes Yahweh's grace to Israel but culminates in a very careful, tactful reminder to Israel of her role as the covenant people. In this indirect way, therefore, the formula "I, I am He" functions not only to proclaim Yahweh's grace but also to remind Israel of the totality of her life as the covenant people.

Our analysis of the formula "I am He" suggests that II Isaiah uses it with the same range of meanings that it had in previous tradition. In Deut. 32:39 -- the only passage where the formula occurs apart from the writings of II Isaiah -- the formula functioned within the context of an _apologia_ to express the uniqueness of Yahweh, his sovereignty over history, his grace toward Israel, and his expectation that Israel would fulfill her responsibilities as his covenant people. II Isaiah uses the formula to express all of these meanings. It is especially significant that he uses it to remind his fellow exiles that Yahweh still calls them to be a faithful and obedient covenant people. He brings out this theme especially in the trial scene in Is. 43:8-13 and the disputation in Is. 51:9-52:2, but he also alludes to it in the announcements of salvation in Is. 46:1-4 and 52:3-6 and the trial scene in Is. 43:25-28. In these respects II Isaiah preserves the same connotations that the formula has in Deut. 32: 39, even if it must remain uncertain whether he was actually acquainted with this passage.

It is also very significant that II Isaiah uses the formula "I am He" a total of eight times, in marked contrast to the one occurrence elsewhere in the Old Testament. As we saw earlier, he evidently wished to

emphasize that Yahweh alone could speak in this way, in
contrast to the "I style" of monarchs or the "I am"
claims of kingdoms in the Ancient Near East. It is
consistent with this polemical interest that II Isaiah
uses the formula "I am He" when Yahweh is addressing
the other nations of the world in the setting of a trial
scene (Is. 41:1-4; 43:8-13). We should also notice,
however, that he uses the formula most often when
Yahweh is addressing Israel, in an announcement of
salvation (Is. 46:1-4; 48:12-16; 52:3-6), a trial scene
involving Israel herself (Is. 43:25-28), or a disputation with Israel (Is. 51:9-52:2). In this way II Isaiah
wishes to remind his fellow exiles that Yahweh's solemn
assertion "I am He," as polemical as it may be in
relation to the power structures of the ancient world,
is intended, in the final analysis, as a way of
addressing them in their own situation of exile.

CHAPTER V
Concluding Observations

This study has sought to develop the view that
II Isaiah proclaimed a "holistic" message that included
the themes of imminent deliverance and continuing
covenant responsibility -- or, more generally, grace
and law. This concluding section will summarize the
major results of the investigation, beginning with the
ancient world outside the Bible and then continuing
more extensively with Old Testament tradition and with
II Isaiah himself. This concluding section will also
suggest some ways in which the study has significance
for understanding the form of II Isaiah's message, his
concern to address his message to a specific cultural-
political setting, and some parallels between II
Isaiah's message and the structure of New Testament
thought.

A. Extrabiblical Examples

The extrabiblical examples of self-predication
illustrate a general "I am" style of speaking, rather
widespread throughout the Ancient Near East, in which a
god or king identifies himself to his people and relates
his accomplishments. In a very general way it is
possible that II Isaiah was familiar with this rhetorical
style as it was cultivated in his environment, although
it is uncertain exactly which examples he may have been
familiar with. The existence of this "I am" style of
speaking may help explain the relatively high frequency
with which II Isaiah attributes to Yahweh the formulas
"I am Yahweh," "I am God," and "I am He."

The Egyptian myth concerning the supreme god Re
illustrates the importance of the concept of "name" as

an expression of inner reality and personal identity.
The idea of "name" has this same significance in the
self-predication "I am Yahweh," although there would be
no reason to think of direct influence of this myth on
Old Testament tradition or on II Isaiah specifically.

The Egyptian oracle that Harmakhis, the god in
the Sphinx, addresses to Thutmose IV shows some
interesting parallels to the salvation oracle in II
Isaiah. These include the self-predication of the
deity, the direct address to the recipient, supporting
clauses of reassurance, and a specific promise of
assistance. The Egyptian oracle also incorporates the
motif of human activity, since the god in the Sphinx
asks Thutmose to clear away the encroaching sands of
the desert. By asking Thutmose to accept responsibility
as well as assistance, the oracle presents ideas that
correspond very generally to the Old Testament themes
of covenant obligation and grace. It is interesting,
in contrast, that II Isaiah makes no attempt to incorporate the theme of law or covenant obligation within
the structure of the salvation oracle. All of his
examples of this type of speech (Is. 41:8-13, 14-16;
43:1-3, 4-7; 44:1-5) express only the theme of grace.

The oracles delivered by various divinities to
kings of Syria and Assyria in the eighth and seventh
centuries B.C. also exhibit close parallels in form to
the salvation oracle as II Isaiah uses it. As in the
case of the Egyptian oracle to Thutmose, there is no
reason to suppose that these oracles from Syria and
Assyria were directly known to II Isaiah. They may be
illustrative, however, of a pattern with which he was
acquainted. Unlike the Egyptian oracle, these oracles
from Syria and Assyria do not seem to include requests
or commands that would correspond generally to the

theme of human activity or covenant obligation as it
finds expression in Old Testament tradition.

Extrabiblical parallels also illustrate an "I am"
style of speaking in which human kings asserted their
royal status and power, or cities or countries made
pretentious claims for themselves that were tantamount
to an assumption of divine status and dignity. It is
clear that II Isaiah was familiar with such claims,
since he quotes the assertion of Babylon, "I am, and
there is no one besides me" (Is. 47:8, 10). In a more
general way, II Isaiah was engaging in polemic against
all competing claims to special status and honor when
he attributed "I am" forms of expression to Yahweh
himself.

B. Old Testament Tradition

Early narrative sources (J and E) indicate that
the expression "I am Yahweh" was a very early form of
divine self-predication that had its original setting
in God's revelation of himself to Moses. From the
beginning, this self-predication functioned to communicate the themes of both grace and law as constitutive
elements in Israel's understanding of Yahweh and her
understanding of herself as the covenant people. The
self-predication introduced Yahweh as the God who freely
took the initiative to deliver Israel from bondage, and
it also presented him as the God who expected Israel to
fulfill her religious and ethical responsibilities
within the covenant relationship.

The prophet Hosea provides relatively early
confirmation that the self-predication "I am Yahweh"
had its original setting in the time of Moses and that
it embraces the themes of both grace and law. The

parallelism between Hos. 13:4 and the introduction to
the Ten Commandments in Ex. 20:2, which may come from
the E document, helps to clarify the relationship
between grace and law. It indicates that grace precedes
law, and the acceptance of law is the response to grace.

The P document clarifies and systematizes the
ideas of earlier sources, associating the formula "I am
Yahweh" with several distinct motifs -- the original
revelation of the divine name to Moses, the communication of this revelation to the people of Israel, the
activity of God in history on behalf of his people, the
covenant relationship between God and his people, and
the close correlation between the themes of grace and
law. The P document uses "I am Yahweh" and "I am Yahweh
your God" with the same meaning, connecting both forms
of self-predication with both themes, grace and law.

The Holiness Code in Lev. 17-26 usually employs
the formula "I am Yahweh" at the close of a commandment
that Yahweh gives to Moses, with the expectation that
Moses will teach it to the people of Israel. In this
position the self-predication serves primarily to
emphasize the divine source and authority of the
commandment. The Holiness Code, however, also uses "I
am Yahweh" in a number of passages that combine the
themes of Exodus deliverance and covenant obligation,
or grace and law. Like the P document in Ex. 6:6-7,
the Holiness Code occasionally brings out the close
connection between "I am Yahweh" and the covenant
formula, "I will be your God, and you shall be my
people." In its present form, at least, the Holiness
Code uses "I am Yahweh your God" and "I am Yahweh" with
essentially the same meaning, even if the longer formula
sometimes emphasizes God's gracious activity on behalf
of Israel, and the shorter formula sometimes emphasizes

his expectation that Israel will fulfill her covenant
responsibilities.

The prophet Ezekiel usually uses the shorter
formula, "I am Yahweh," although he sometimes uses "I
am Yahweh your (their) God," and he also employs a
distinctive formula, "I am Yahweh God." There is no
reason to believe that any of these formulas is associated with a specific theme to the exclusion of others.
A more important characteristic of Ezekiel's writing is
that he almost always uses the introductory statement
"you (they) shall know that . . ." before a formula of
divine self-predication. As Zimmerli has pointed out,
this usage indicates that persons are called to respond
in "knowledge" and "acknowledgement" of Yahweh's actions
toward Israel, as he shows grace or judgment to her
throughout her history. Like earlier sources, Ezekiel
associates the self-predication "I am Yahweh" with a
theophany that occurred at the time of Moses and gave
expression to the themes of both grace and law.

Other examples of the self-predication "I am
Yahweh" occur in Deut. 5:6; 29:6; Judg. 6:10; I Kings
20:13, 28; Ps. 81:10; Jer. 9:24; 17:10; 24:7; 32:27.
All of these examples except those in I Kings employ
the formula in connection with the themes of both grace
and law. Some of these occurrences, especially the one
in Ps. 81, suggest that the formula "I am Yahweh" was
preserved in the context of covenant liturgy.

It is also significant that most of the occurrences of "I am Yahweh" in the Old Testament, apart
from II Isaiah, are in three sources -- Ezekiel, the
Holiness Code, and the P document (66, 47, and 19 times,
respectively). These sources have several characteristics in common: they come from the early or the middle
sixth century B.C., they were probably written by exiles

in Babylon, and they all reflect priestly interests.
After the destruction of the temple in 587 B.C. and the
loss of a liturgical setting for the formula "I am
Yahweh," these sources all reflect the need to preserve
the formula in written form until the time would come
when its liturgical context could be restored. The
writers of these sources also wanted to employ the
formula as a way of reassuring themselves and their
readers that Yahweh could indeed be present among them
during their exile in a foreign land. With their
priestly backgrounds, finally, these writers were
especially interested in the history of the formula
"I am Yahweh," its relation to the themes of grace and
law, and its preservation in a cultic setting.

The self-predication "I am Yahweh" also occurs
in several sources that may be assigned to post-exilic
times (Is. 27:3; 60:16, 22; 61:8; Joel 2:27; 3:17;
Zech. 10:6). These instances are important primarily
because they represent a continuation of themes that
appeared in earlier Old Testament tradition. These
examples all express the idea of Yahweh's blessing and
protection for his people, and some of them also express
the idea of covenant responsibility on the part of the
people.

The self-predication "I am God" is similar in
several respects to "I am Yahweh." Both formulas
originated in theophanies to individual persons, and in
later times both were preserved in the setting of temple
worship. Both could also express the theme of grace,
at least in the general sense that God promised to take
some initiative to help his people according to their
situation at the time.

The formula "I am God," on the other hand, also
shows several important differences from "I am Yahweh."

Evidently because the words for "God" are more general
in reference, and thus less suitable for use in divine
self-predication, "I am God" occurs only ten times in
the Old Testament, apart from II Isaiah, in contrast to
160 occurrences for "I am Yahweh." The formula "I am
God" derives from the patriarchal period, beginning with
the divine revelation to Abraham, whereas "I am Yahweh"
derives from God's revelation of himself to Moses. In
content, the self-predication "I am God" almost always
expresses the theme of grace -- God's promises to his
people, the blessing of his presence, or the benefits
of his action. The occurrences of "I am Yahweh," on the
other hand, almost always reflect a creative tension
between the themes of grace and law, as these originally
found expression in the Exodus from Egypt and in Israel's
obligations under the terms of the Sinai covenant.

The third form of divine self-predication in Old
Testament tradition is the succinct formula "I am He."
This evidently occurs only in Deut. 32:39, where it
expresses, in the context of the poem, the uniqueness
of Yahweh as the sole God, his sovereignty over the
course of history, his grace toward his people Israel,
and his expectation that they would fulfill their
covenant obligations. Comparable expressions in Jer.
14:22; Ps. 102:27; and Josh. 23:3, 10 help to illumine
the meaning of "I am He," although these other
expressions do not employ the first person singular.

C. The Content of II Isaiah's Message

This study has supported the thesis that II
Isaiah did not simply preach a message of deliverance
from exile. He did of course emphasize salvation or
deliverance as a central theme in his preaching to his

fellow exiles in Babylon. But he also thought of
Israel as a covenant community that still had the
obligation to follow the religious and ethical tenets
of the type represented by the Sinai covenant. In very
careful, tactful ways -- such as the use of the formula
"I am Yahweh" -- II Isaiah reminded his audience that
they were still called to live as a community of
covenant responsibility. As he looked forward to
restoration from exile, he expected that Israel would
continue to live as this covenant community. He also
expected that Israel would enlarge her sense of covenant
obligation to accept the role of serving as a "covenant
to the people, a light to the nations" (Is. 42:6).

Our study of II Isaiah has actually approached
the prophet's writings from three points of view --
it has analyzed the meaning of the different forms of
divine self-predication ("I am Yahweh," "I am God," and
"I am He"), it has examined different types of passages,
and it has sought to identify specific themes that II
Isaiah was presenting. By way of summary, it may be
helpful to list these themes and then indicate their
patterns of distribution in connection with the several
forms of self-predication and the various types of
passages. It is possible to identify nine distinct
themes that II Isaiah presents in this way:

1. Yahweh is the sole God in the world.
2. Yahweh is the incomparable God; there
   is none like him.
3. Yahweh is active in history and sovereign
   over the course of history.
4. Yahweh is guiding the successful career
   of Cyrus of Persia.
5. Yahweh is about to deliver Israel from
   exile and captivity.

6. Yahweh is the Creator of all things.
7. Yahweh is the Creator of Israel.
8. Yahweh still calls Israel to be his
   covenant people and fulfill the religious
   and ethical responsibilities of the kind
   represented by the Sinai covenant.
9. Yahweh also calls Israel to enlarge her
   understanding of covenant responsibility
   by becoming "a light to the nations."

It is clear that some of these themes are closely
related to others. The idea that Yahweh is active in
history, for example, underlies the belief that he is
guiding the career of Cyrus, and this in turn leads to
the thought that he is about to deliver his people from
exile. Within the context of II Isaiah's message to
his fellow exiles, all three of these ideas express the
general theme of Yahweh's "grace" to his people Israel.
In contrast, the last two themes in the list above
represent the general idea of "law," in the sense that
Yahweh asks Israel to accept obligations as his covenant
people. He still calls her to fulfill religious and
ethical responsibilities, and he also calls her to
enlarge her understanding of her role on the scene of
world history.

The following table gives the distribution of
these themes, identified by the same numbers as in the
list above:

"I am Yahweh" -- themes
    trial scene: Yahweh and the nations
        41:1-4   1   3 4 5
        43:8-13   1   2   3   5   8

salvation oracle
    41:8-13   3   5
    43:1-3   3   5   7
announcement of salvation
    43:14-21   3   5   7 8
hymn of self-praise
    44:24-28   1   3 4 5 6 7
    45:18-19   1   3   6   8
disputation with Israel
    49:14-26   3   5
    51:9-52:2   3   5 6 7 8
charge to Israel
    42:5-9   2   3   6   8 9
    48:17-19   3   5   8 (9)
address to Cyrus
    45:1-8   1 2 3 4 5 6   9

"I am God" -- themes
    trial scene: Yahweh and the nations
        43:8-13   1 2 3   5   8
    salvation oracle
        41:8-13   3   5
    disputation with Israel
        46:8-13   1 2 3 4 5   8
    address to the nations
        45:22-23   1   3   9

"I am He" -- themes
    trial scene: Yahweh and the nations
        41:1-4   1   3 4 5
        43:8-13   1 2 3   5   8

announcement of salvation

46:1-4	1	3		5	(8)
48:12-16	1	3	4	5	6
52:3-6		3		5	(8)

trial scene: Yahweh and Israel

43:25-28	3	5	(8)

disputation with Israel

51:9-52:2	3		5	6	7 8

Although some uncertainty may exist about details, a table of this kind has value in summarizing the analysis of II Isaiah's writings that the present study has undertaken and clarifying relationships among forms of self-predication, types of passages, and conceptual motifs. The belief that Yahweh is the sole God is a general presupposition of II Isaiah's thought that he does not try to express in every passage or literary unit. The table includes this theme only when the prophet makes it explicit. The table gives some numbers in parentheses to indicate that these themes seem to be implied in the context, although they are not stated directly. Sometimes, for example, II Isaiah indicates that he is thinking holistically, in terms of the entire life-span of Israel from beginning to end, and not just in terms of the immediate future with the deliverance that it will bring. When II Isaiah thinks of the entire course of Israel's life, it is very likely that he has in mind all the significant events in her history and all the significant aspects of her relationship to Yahweh.

The theme that occurs most frequently in this table is number 3 -- the belief that Yahweh is active in history and sovereign over the course of history. II Isaiah expresses this theme in every passage in

which he employs a divine self-predication, regardless
of the specific type of self-predication or the form
critical category to which the passage belongs. The
frequency of this theme illustrates its central importance in II Isaiah's understanding of Yahweh. It also
illustrates the basic importance of "grace" in the
prophet's view of Yahweh, since the theme of Yahweh's
sovereignty over history becomes a way of reassuring
the exiles that Yahweh is indeed able to deliver them
from captivity.

It is also significant that theme number 5 occurs
almost as often as number 3. Number 5 follows closely
from number 3. It indicates more specifically that
Yahweh is about to intervene in history on behalf of
Israel, and it becomes now a more direct expression of
Yahweh's grace toward his people. This theme appears
regularly with all three types of self-predication,
with no significant difference in proportion of occurrence. The theme also appears in almost all the
different types of passages, being absent only in the
address to the nations (Is. 45:22-23).

Themes 1, 2, and 4 appear less often in the
passages with which this study deals. It is interesting that they do occur in connection with all three
forms of divine self-predication. When numbers 1 and 2
occur together, they usually do so in passages in which
Yahweh is addressing Gentile people -- i.e., trial
scenes between Yahweh and the nations, and Yahweh's
address to Cyrus. These are the contexts in which II
Isaiah would want to emphasize that Yahweh is the sole
God and the incomparable God. II Isaiah utilizes theme
number 4 in passages in which Yahweh is addressing
Gentile peoples and also passages in which he is
addressing Israel. Both kinds of passage provide

appropriate settings for II Isaiah to affirm that
Yahweh is guiding the successful career of Cyrus.

It is interesting too that references to Yahweh's
role as Creator of all things and Creator of Israel
(themes 6 and 7) are not very frequent in the passages
that we have examined. II Isaiah, in general, was more
concerned with Yahweh's role as Lord of history than
his role as Creator. When he depicted Yahweh as
Creator, he usually did so as a way of supporting the
belief in him as Lord of history. It may be significant,
however, that II Isaiah refers to Yahweh as Creator in
connection with the self-predications "I am Yahweh" and
"I am He," but not "I am God." Because the words for
"God" -- el and elohim -- were sometimes used to refer
to other deities, some of whom were believed to have
functions in creation, II Isaiah may have wished to
avoid possible confusion at this point.

From the standpoint of our present study, the
most significant point illustrated by the table above
is that themes number 8 and 9 appear a number of times
in connection with formulas of divine self-predication.
Number 8 -- the affirmation that Yahweh still calls
Israel to live as a covenant people -- occurs in
connection with all three forms of self-predication.
It also occurs in a variety of different types of
passages -- the trial scene between Yahweh and the
nations, the announcement of salvation, the hymn of
self-praise, the disputation with Israel, the charge to
Israel, and probably also the trial scene between
Yahweh and Israel. This pattern of distribution, in
connection with different forms of self-predication and
different types of passage, supports the view that the
theme of covenant responsibility played an essential
part in the structure of II Isaiah's thought. Theme

number 9 -- the belief that Yahweh calls Israel to be
"a light to the nations" -- is less widely attested,
but it does occur in connection with two forms of self-
predication and in several different types of passage.
These data concerning the occurrences of themes 8 and 9
all support the argument of the present study that II
Isaiah proclaimed a message of both "grace" and "law,"
imminent deliverance and continuing covenant responsibility.

When II Isaiah connects the self-predication "I
am Yahweh" with a reminder to Israel of her covenant
responsibility, he is employing the self-predication in
a way that he had evidently become familiar with from
Old Testament tradition. As we saw in our survey of
Old Testament sources, the formula "I am Yahweh" had
been connected from the beginning with the themes of
grace and law, and it maintained this connection
throughout the Old Testament period. In a similar way,
when II Isaiah employs "I am He" to express the idea of
covenant obligation, he is using it in connection with
a theme that it had expressed previously. In contrast,
it is especially interesting that II Isaiah uses the
formula "I am God" with a new emphasis. In previous
Old Testament usage this self-predication occurred only
ten times, almost always as a way of expressing the
grace that God was bestowing on his people. II Isaiah
uses the formula four times within a relatively brief
collection of writings. In all four instances the
formula expresses the idea of grace, but in three of
these occurrences it also refers to Israel's role and
responsibility as the covenant people. It is uncertain
whether II Isaiah intentionally sought to modify the
connotations of the formula "I am God," or whether he
did not realize that he was using it with a new and

unexpected emphasis. In either case, his usage reflects
the pervasive influence of the ideas of grace and law
in the texture of his thought.

II Isaiah's references to the theme of covenant
responsibility, in connection with all three forms of
divine self-predication and in different types of
passages, also corroborate the validity of the methodology of the present study. As it was explained in the
Preface, the study rests on the assumption that a basic
formula such as "I am Yahweh" will acquire specific
connotations (in this case, the motifs of grace and
law) and then will retain these through changing
historical circumstances (in this case, the fall of
Jerusalem, the loss of a liturgical context in temple
worship, and the exile to Babylon). This assumption
functions as the "warrant" in supporting the view that
the formula still had these connotations for II Isaiah
and his audience. Although the concept of "warrant" is
valid, it should not have to bear too much interpretive
weight by itself. The analysis of II Isaiah's writings,
as he proclaims his message in connection with different
forms of self-predication and different types of literary
units, gives exegetical confirmation for the conclusion
to which the warrant points, that "grace" and "law" were
integral aspects of the prophet's thought.

D. The Form of II Isaiah's Message

In the strictest sense the present study is
thematic rather than form critical, for it has sought
to analyze the meaning of formulas of divine self-
predication with special attention to their significance
for understanding the relationship between the themes
of grace and law in II Isaiah. It has been convenient,

however, to examine these formulas of self-predication
as they appear in different kinds of passages in II
Isaiah, and in this respect the study has used the
method of form critical analysis. In this section we
may look briefly at some of the results of the study as
they relate to the method of form criticism.

        The study has brought out the point, for example,
that a passage may have a double audience -- a "direct"
audience to which the verses are ostensibly addressed,
and then also an "indirect" one for which II Isaiah may
actually have composed the passage. The trial scenes
between Yahweh and the nations of the world (Is. 41:1-4;
43:8-13) are cast in the form of a summons to the
nations, yet at the same time they are directed to
Israel as she "listens in" and applies the message to
her own situation. Although II Isaiah was indeed concerned about the nations of the world, his immediate
purpose in composing these trial scenes was to reassure
Israel, the indirect audience, that Yahweh was the
sovereign Lord of history who was about to deliver his
people from exile. In a similar way the address to
Cyrus (Is. 45:1-8) and the address to the nations (Is.
45:22-23) are also directed to Israel as ways of assuring her of imminent deliverance and reminding her of
her role as the covenant people of Yahweh.

        The study has also suggested that II Isaiah could
incorporate the theme of covenant obligation into certain
types of passages that would not seem able, at first
sight, to accommodate this theme. It is significant
that II Isaiah could insert this theme in a trial scene
between Yahweh and the nations (Is. 43:8-13), an
announcement of salvation (Is. 43:14-21; 46:1-4; 52:
3-6), a hymn of self-praise (Is. 45:18-19), a disputation
with Israel (Is. 46:8-13; 51:9-52:2), and an address to

Cyrus (Is. 45:1-8). These are all passages which would
be expected to bring, directly or indirectly, a message
of salvation for Israel, but not a reminder of law or
covenant obligation. The fact that II Isaiah could
utilize them as vehicles for presenting the theme of
covenant obligation indicates that he felt a certain
freedom in handling the different types of form critical
units that were available to him. In terms of theological outlook, it reflects also his concern to bring a
holistic message that included the themes of both grace
and law.

A final observation concerning form criticism
deals with the importance of identifying the relationship of different form critical units to one another.
As the analysis of II Isaiah's writings in Chapter IV
has suggested, it is significant that a trial scene
between Yahweh and the nations (Is. 41:1-4) precedes a
salvation oracle (Is. 41:8-13); a "reproach" (Is. 42:
18-25) precedes a salvation oracle (Is. 43:1-3); a
reference to Cyrus is always followed by a reference to
Israel (Is. 41:1-4 and 41:8-16; Is. 41:21-29 and 42:1-9;
Is. 48:12-16 and 48:17-19, etc.); an announcement of
salvation to Israel (Is. 48:12-16) is followed by a
charge to Israel (Is. 48:17-19), and both together
prepare the way for the instructions to depart from
Babylon (Is. 48:20-21); a trial scene between Yahweh
and Israel (Is. 43:25-28) precedes a salvation oracle
(Is. 44:1-5). The previous analysis of these passages
has indicated some of the ways in which the arrangement
of units establishes a context that contributes to the
interpretation of an individual passage. The trial
scene between Yahweh and Israel, for example, reminds
Israel how grievously she has erred in the past; this
reminder, in turn, makes it all the more remarkable that

the trial scene is followed by a salvation oracle in
which Yahweh assures Israel that he still cares about
her and will soon deliver her from captivity (Is. 43:
25-28; 44:1-5).

E. The Prophetic Word in its Setting

In several ways the "cultural-political setting"
must be taken into account in any analysis of the processes by which the words of Scripture came into being
and then are later interpreted. The original writer
(in this case, II Isaiah) speaks out of his own setting,
bringing an authentic word from God as he understands
it and finds it meaningful in the circumstances of his
own time and place. The original writer also addresses
readers (in this case, the exiles in Babylon) who stand
in their own cultural-political setting and want to
understand the writer's message in relation to their
own situation. The circumstances of the writer may be
different from those of his readers. In the case of II
Isaiah, who was one of the exiles in Babylon, the
situations of writer and readers were the same. In any
case, the writer accepts the task of bringing a genuine
message from God, understanding it as it addresses him
in his own cultural-political setting, and then stating
it as it addresses his readers in their setting. For
a prophet like II Isaiah, this task would have been
essentially the same whether he put his words in writing
from the very beginning, or whether he delivered them
orally at first and then wrote them down at a later
time and arranged them in their present form.
Analogous processes will take place in later
times whenever an interpreter seeks to understand the
meaning of Scripture in relation to the cultural-

political settings that exist in his own day. The whole
procedure becomes more complicated, however, because
the interpreter must take account of the original contexts as well as those of his own time. In ascertaining
the meaning of Scripture for himself, the interpreter
must ask what the "word" from God meant to the original
writer and the original audience in their cultural-
political settings, and then in the light of these
original meanings he can ask how this word addresses
him in his own setting. If an interpreter seeks to
understand the meaning of Scripture for an audience in
a cultural-political setting different from his own --
if someone in the "first world," for example, asks what
Scripture means for those in the "third world" -- he
must engage in a similar process of correlating the
original situations with a set of circumstances in his
own day. Throughout all of these processes, the
assumption is not that the meaning of Scripture changes
as it relates itself to different cultural and political
conditions, but that the word of God in Scripture does
address persons in the concrete circumstances of their
lives.

When we examine the themes of "grace" and "law"
in II Isaiah, we find that the prophet did formulate
his message with regard to the cultural-political
situation of his audience. He knew that his fellow
exiles still felt grief and humiliation from the loss
of their country nearly half a century earlier. He was
also aware of their feeling that Yahweh would not, or
could not, come to their aid now and deliver them from
exile. He evidently thought too that it would serve no
constructive purpose merely to reiterate Israel's many
failures in the past. II Isaiah must have taken all
these factors into consideration when he formulated his

message to his fellow exiles. He emphasized his joyful
conviction that Yahweh would soon come to deliver them,
and he reassured them that they had suffered enough for
their wrongdoings in the past.

At the same time, it is significant that II
Isaiah was also concerned to preserve the integrity or
wholeness of the prophetic word that he was commissioned
to bring to the community of exiles. He knew that his
message must include the theme of "law" as well as
"grace" -- partly because he knew that both themes had
informed the history of his people, partly because he
stood in the tradition of the pre-exilic prophets, and
partly, we must assume, because he recognized both
themes as essential elements in the message that God
had called him to deliver. With unusual sensitivity
and tact -- evident especially in his use of the solemn
formula "I am Yahweh," which conveyed an awareness of
both grace and law -- II Isaiah reminded the exiles
that Yahweh was coming to deliver them and to call them
to himself as his covenant people. Although he formulated his message with regard to the situation of his
audience, he did not regard it as merely relative to a
particular situation. With a sense of responsibility
to his heritage, together with a sensitive concern for
the feelings of his audience, he formulated his message
and presented it in its intrinsic integrity.

At this point we can perceive another aspect of
II Isaiah's attitude toward the situation of his
audience. He did not simply relate his prophetic word
to their cultural-political setting, as important as
this effort was in the process of communication. At a
more profound level, he also addressed the prophetic
word to his audience in terms of their relationship to
God, which defined their identity as the people of God

and provided the perspective, in turn, from which they
could assess the significance of their cultural-
political environment. As a result of his concern for
the wholeness of the prophetic word, II Isaiah was able
to relate his message to the situation of his audience
in such a way that the situation, in turn, could be
related to the message.

II Isaiah's concern for the wholeness of the
prophetic word suggests that the interpreter of
Scripture today can identify a similar relationship
between "word" and "situation." The interpreter seeks
to understand the message of Scripture as it was
formulated in relation to the original situations of
the writer and his audience, and as it has significance
for the interpreter himself in his own cultural-
political setting. As a further step, the interpreter
can ask how the word of Scripture can define and inform
his own relationship to God, from which, in turn, he
acquires perspective in assessing the significance of
a given cultural-political setting. As in the case of
II Isaiah, the word of Scripture today can relate itself to a human situation in such a way that the
situation, in turn, can be fully understood only in the
light of the word.

F. Parallels to New Testament Thought

Like II Isaiah, Jesus also proclaimed a message
that included the themes of both grace and law. In his
preaching, for example, the proclamation of the gospel
-- the "good news" that God was bringing his kingdom
and was making it available to all who recognized their
need for it -- represented the theme of grace. Jesus'
ethical teachings, on the other hand, gave examples of

ways in which his followers should live as members of
the new covenant community that he was establishing.
Neither theme, grace or law, can be isolated from the
other in the structure of Jesus' message. When Jesus
ate a meal with tax collectors and sinners, he was
utilizing the imagery of the messianic banquet to
symbolize God's gracious offer of his kingdom (Mk. 2:
15-17). Although he did not speak of covenant obligation at this point, Jesus certainly assumed that the
tax collectors and sinners would make an appropriate
ethical response if they wished to become his followers.
As he indicated on another occasion, eating and drinking
with him would mean nothing if sinners did not change
their way of life (Lk. 13:26-27). Conversely, Jesus'
teachings such as those in the Sermon on the Mount
represent the theme of law, but law does not stand in
isolation as an ethical requirement by itself. God's
gracious offer of his kingdom is always presupposed as
the context for the ethical requirements of life in the
new covenant community. As Jeremias especially has
pointed out, God's "gift" of the kingdom always precedes
the "demand" that the followers of Jesus obey the
teachings of the Sermon on the Mount.[82]

The apostle Paul, although he used different
terminology, also taught that God's grace precedes and
evokes the response of ethical activity. God's redemptive work through Christ, Paul believed, means that
both Jews and Gentiles are "justified by his grace as a
gift" (Rom. 3:24). Paul went on to argue that justifi-
cation does not allow an antinomian response -- "to
continue in sin that grace may abound" (Rom. 6:1).
Rather it signifies a dying to sin, represented by
baptism, so that the Christian "might walk in newness
of life" (Rom. 6:4) and become "alive to God in Christ

Jesus" (Rom. 6:11). In other contexts Paul uses a
different vocabulary to express his message of grace
and law. When he speaks of "faith working through love"
(Gal. 5:6), he means that the Christian receives God's
grace in faith, and then expresses his new relationship
with God through deeds of loving service to others (cf.
Gal. 5:13-14). When he says, "If we live by the Spirit,
let us also walk by the Spirit" (Gal. 5:25), he employs
a different terminology again to indicate that
Christians have received the gift of God's grace and
are expected now to make the ethical response of living
according to God's will (cf. Gal. 5:22-23). In all
these ways Paul reflects the same perspective as II
Isaiah and Jesus himself, that God's "grace" precedes
"law" and then entails law in the sense of the ethical
response of the covenant community.

     In a very similar way the writer of the letter
to the Ephesians -- whether this was Paul or some other
early Christian -- reminds his readers, "by grace you
have been saved through faith" (Eph. 2:8). He
emphasizes that they were not saved "because of works"
(Eph. 2:9), but he goes on to point out that they were
"created in Christ Jesus for good works" (Eph. 2:10).
In this way the writer expresses his conviction that
God's grace precedes human ethical activity; he also
wants to emphasize that it is part of God's purpose for
human life that ethical activity should be a response
to grace. To look at one further example from the New
Testament, we may note that the writer of the First
Letter of John, with his genius for simplicity and
clarity of thought, has perhaps given the best statement
of the relationship between grace and covenant responsibility: "Beloved, if God so loved us, we also ought to
love one another" (I John 4:11; cf. 4:19).

In significant ways such as these, the integral
relationship between grace and law, which developed in
early Old Testament tradition and then governed the
thought of II Isaiah, continued to inform the structure
of New Testament faith and proclamation.

NOTES

[1] Claus Westermann, _Isaiah 40-66_, The Old Testament Library (Philadelphia: The Westminster Press, 1969), p. 9. Westermann's comment echoes the remark of Hugo Gressmann that II Isaiah gives only promises (_Verheissungen_) that speak of salvation (_Heil_) rather than threats (_Drohungen_) that warn of disaster (_Unheil_); cf. "Die literarische Analyse Deuterojesajas," _Zeitschrift für die alttestamentliche Wissenschaft_ 34 (1914), pp. 268-69. In the context of the present study the important question is not simply the relation between salvation and disaster, but the relation between grace and covenant obligation.

[2] Walther Eichrodt, _Theology of the Old Testament_ (London: SCM Press Ltd, 1961), I, p. 61.

[3] James Muilenburg, "The Book of Isaiah: Chapters 40-66," _The Interpreter's Bible_ (New York and Nashville: Abingdon Press, 1966), V, p. 405.

[4] Ibid., p. 400.

[5] Ibid., p. 466.

[6] John L. McKenzie, S.J., _Second Isaiah_, The Anchor Bible, Vol. 20 (Garden City, New York: Doubleday & Company, Inc., 1968), p. LVII.

[7] Ibid., p. LX.

[8] Ibid., p. LXII.

[9] As a working hypothesis, II Isaiah's writings are understood here to consist of Is. 40-55. In contrast to the frequency with which self-predications occur in these chapters, it may be noted that "I am Yahweh" occurs elsewhere in Isaiah only in 27:3; 60:16, 22; 61:8; "I am God" and "I am He" do not occur in the book of Isaiah apart from chs. 40-55.

[10] From "The God and His Unknown Name of Power," trans. John A. Wilson, in _Ancient Near Eastern Texts Relating to the Old Testament_, 2nd ed., ed. James B. Pritchard (Princeton: Princeton University Press, 1955), p. 13.

[11] From "Another Version of the Creation by Atum," trans. John A. Wilson, in Pritchard, op. cit., pp. 3-4.

[12] From "A Divine Oracle Through a Dream," trans.
John A. Wilson, in Pritchard, op. cit., p. 449.

[13] This oracle and the preceding one are from
"Zakir of Hamat and Lu'ath," trans. Franz Rosenthal, in
Pritchard, op. cit., p. 501.

[14] From "Oracles Concerning Esarhaddon," trans.
Robert H. Pfeiffer, in Pritchard, op. cit., p. 449.
For the self-predication of Ishtar in a hymn of self-
praise, cf. also the "Hymn to Ishtar" in Robert William
Rogers, Cuneiform Parallels to the Old Testament (New
York: Eaton & Mains; Cincinnati: Jennings & Graham,
1912), pp. 162-63.

[15] Cf. Pritchard, op. cit., pp. 450-51.

[16] From "The Legend of Sargon," trans. E.A.
Speiser, in Pritchard, op. cit., p. 119. For the self-
predication of the war god Ningirsu in an address to
Gudea (ca. 2340 B.C.) cf. Eduard Norden, Agnostos Theos
(Leipzig and Berlin: B.G. Teubner, 1923), p. 211.
Norden points out that the "I am" form of predication
was originally restricted to gods but was later trans-
ferred to kings, as their earthly representatives
(p. 214).

[17] From "The Code of Hammurabi," trans. Theophile
J. Meek, in Pritchard, op. cit., p. 164.

[18] Cf. Pritchard, op. cit., pp. 276, 320, 499-501.
For the self-predication of Nebuchadnezzar of Babylon,
in an inscription in which he relates, e.g., how he
built the Ishtar gate, cf. Stephen Langdon, Die neubabylonischen Königsinschriften (Leipzig: J.C. Hinrichs,
1912), p. 191.

[19] From "Cyrus," trans. A. Leo Oppenheim, in
Pritchard, op. cit., p. 316.

[20] The following types of clauses have been counted
in determining this total: 1) nominal clauses in which
"Yahweh" is clearly predicate -- e.g., ani Yahweh, Ex.
6:2, "I am Yahweh"; 2) nominal clauses in which "Yahweh"
is probably predicate, although it could be construed
as appositive to the subject -- e.g., ani Yahweh
elohekem, Ex. 16:12, "I am Yahweh your God," or possibly
"I, Yahweh, am your God"; also ani Yahweh meqaddishkem,
Lev. 20:8, "I am Yahweh, who sanctify you," or possibly
"I, Yahweh, sanctify you."

The following types of clauses have not been
included: 1) nominal clauses in which "Yahweh" is
probably appositive to "I" -- e.g., anoki Yahweh eloheka
el qanna, Ex. 20:5, "I, Yahweh your God, am a jealous
God"; also qadosh ani Yahweh elohekem, Lev. 19:2,
literally "Holy am I, Yahweh your God"; 2) apparent
nominal clauses in which "Yahweh" is most probably
appositive to "I" -- e.g., halo anoki Yahweh, Ex. 4:11,
"Is it not I, Yahweh, (who do these things)?"; 3) verbal
clauses, in which Yahweh is appositive to "I," the
subject of a finite verb -- e.g., ani Yahweh dibbarti,
Ezek. 5:13, "I, Yahweh, have spoken."
    For a discussion of issues in translating self-
predication formulas in Ex. 20:2, the Holiness Code,
and Ezekiel, cf. Walther Zimmerli, "Ich bin Jahwe," in
Gottes Offenbarung: Gesammelte Aufsätze, Theologische
Bücherei 19 (München: Chr. Kaiser Verlag, 1963), pp.
11-40, especially 11-17. Zimmerli argues, for instance,
that "I am Yahweh" and "I am Yahweh your God" clearly
come from the same root, and for this reason the longer
formula must be translated "I am Yahweh your God" rather
than "I, Yahweh, am your God" (p. 14). In expressions
such as "I, Yahweh your God, am holy," Zimmerli notes
that the original structure of the self-predication has
been broken apart so that the name Yahweh is "degraded"
from predicate to attribute of the subject (p. 15).
Even in such cases, however, he makes the important
observation that there are "overtones" of the early
formula, "I am Yahweh" (p. 16).

21 Gen. 15:7; 28:13; Ex. 6:2, 6, 7, 8, 29; 7:5, 17;
8:22; 10:2; 12:12; 14:4, 18; 15:26; 16:12; 29:46 (bis);
31:13; Lev. 11:44, 45; 18:2, 4, 5, 6, 21, 30; 19:3, 4,
10, 12, 14, 16, 18, 25, 28, 30, 31, 32, 34, 36, 37;
20:7, 8, 24; 21:12, 15, 23; 22:2, 3, 8, 9, 16, 30, 31,
32, 33; 23:22, 43; 24:22; 25:17, 38, 55; 26:1, 2, 13,
44, 45; Num. 3:13, 41, 45; 10:10; 15:41 (bis); Deut.
29:6 (Heb. 29:5); Judg. 6:10; I Kings 20:13, 28; Is.
27:3; 60:16, 22; 61:8; Jer. 9:24 (Heb. 9:23); 17:10;
24:7; 32:27; Ezek. 6:7, 10, 13, 14; 7:4, 9, 27; 11:10,
12; 12:15, 16, 20; 13:14, 21, 23; 14:8; 15:7; 16:62;
20:5, 7, 12, 19, 20, 26, 38, 42, 44; 22:16; 24:27;
25:5, 7, 11, 17; 26:6; 28:22, 23, 26; 29:6, 9, 21;
30:8, 19, 25, 26; 32:15; 33:29; 34:27; 35:4, 9, 15;
36:11, 23, 38; 37:6, 13, 28; 38:23; 39:6, 7, 22, 28;
Joel 2:27; 3:17 (Heb. 4:17); Zech. 10:6.

22 Ezek. 13:9; 23:49; 24:24; 28:24; 29:16.

23 Ex. 20:2; Deut. 5:6; Ps. 81:10 (Heb. 81:11);
Hos. 12:9 (Heb. 12:10); 13:4.

[24] The source analysis follows that of Otto
Eissfeldt, The Old Testament: An Introduction (New York
and Evanston: Harper & Row, Publishers, 1965), pp. 188
ff., 233 ff. In addition to J and E, Eissfeldt also
posits a "lay source" (L). He attributes Gen. 15:7;
28:13 to J; Ex. 20:2 to E; Ex. 15:26 to L; Ex. 7:17;
8:22; 10:2 to J or E; Ex. 14:4, 18 to L, J. or E.

[25] In the Old Testament the statement "I am Yahweh"
appears first in Gen. 15:7 and 28:13, the accounts of
the covenant given to Abraham and Jacob. These passages
both belong to the J document. Since the author of J
wished to demonstrate that Yahweh had been worshipped
by name from the early beginnings of human history (cf.
Gen. 4:26), it is very likely that he was responsible
for the use of the term Yahweh in Gen. 15:7 and 28:13.
Apart from these two passages, the self-predication
"I am Yahweh" does not occur in Genesis.

[26] Cf. Gen. 15:7; 28:13, which reflect the usage of
J even if they do not accurately represent the conditions of the pre-Mosaic period. Cf. also Ex. 7:17;
8:22; 10:2; 14:4, 18. These verses all have "I am
Yahweh"; they may come from J or from other early
narrative sources (cf. note 24).

[27] For the view that "I am Yahweh" and "I am Yahweh
your God" have different emphases or meanings in the
Holiness Code (Lev. 17-26), cf. Karl Elliger, "Ich bin
der Herr -- euer Gott," in Kleine Schriften zum Alten
Testament, Theologische Bücherei 32 (München: Chr.
Kaiser Verlag, 1966), pp. 211-31. Elliger notes,
however, that the earliest sources do not show any
essential difference in meaning between the shorter and
the longer formulas: "The Yahwist can employ the simple
formula in the same way as the Elohist or Hosea employs
the expanded one" (p. 230). Elliger also believes that
the P document (more specifically, the so-called
Grundschrift of P) makes no distinction in theological
content between the two formulas (p. 228).

[28] On the relation between the Sinai theophany and
the tabernacle tradition cf. Brevard S. Childs, The Book
of Exodus: a Critical, Theological Commentary
(Philadelphia: The Westminster Press, 1974), pp. 536 ff.
With reference especially to the significance of the
technical term "dwell," Childs believes that "God is
continually present in the portable tabernacle" (p. 540).
For a different view, cf. the comment by John Gray in
The Interpreter's One-Volume Commentary on the Bible,

ed. Charles M. Laymon (Nashville & New York: Abingdon
Press, 1971), p. 60: "Evidently the promise of God's
dwelling in the tabernacle is to be understood in this
sense of his occasional presence in the place of meeting
rather than a localization of the transcendent God of
postexilic Judaism (cf. I Kings 8:27)." Childs' view
would undoubtedly appear to be correct in the sense that
the priestly writer would want to emphasize the per-
manence of God's gracious presence with his people
without necessarily limiting God's presence to the
tabernacle itself.

[29] Cf. Otto Eissfeldt, op. cit., pp. 233-39,
especially p. 238.

[30] On the blessings and curses of ancient treaties
and their parallels in the Old Testament, cf. Delbert
R. Hillers, Covenant: The History of a Biblical Idea
(Baltimore: The Johns Hopkins Press, 1969), especially
chapters 2 and 6.

[31] "I am Yahweh," Lev. 22:33; 26:45. "I am Yahweh
your God," Lev. 19:36; 20:24; 23:43; 25:38, 55; 26:13,
44.

[32] "I am Yahweh," Lev. 18:5, 6, 21; 19:12, 14, 16,
18, 28, 30, 32, 37; 20:8; 21:12, 15, 23; 22:2, 3, 8, 9,
16, 30, 31, 32; 26:2. "I am Yahweh your God," Lev. 18:
2, 4, 30; 19:3, 4, 10, 25, 31, 34; 20:7; 23:22; 24:22;
25:17; 26:1.

[33] Karl Elliger (note 27) has argued that the two
formulas represent different strata of the text: in the
framework, "I am Yahweh your God" expresses God's
incomprehensible grace in fulfilling his promise to
Abraham and his descendants, while in the older collection of laws (and also in the secondary expansion of
the framework), "I am Yahweh" suggests the idea of
Yahweh as a jealous God who wants his people to worship
him alone and obey his commandments. Even this division
into strata, however, would not seem to account for the
fact that both formulas are used to reinforce the theme
of grace, and both are used to support the theme of law.

[34] Cf. Elliger, op. cit., p. 225.

[35] Cf. Zimmerli, "Ich bin Jahwe," p. 21.

[36] Cf. Walther Zimmerli, "Erkenntnis Gottes nach
dem Buche Ezechiel," in Gottes Offenbarung: Gesammelte

Aufsätze, Theologische Bücherei 19 (München: Chr.
Kaiser Verlag, 1963), pp. 41-119, especially pp. 46-49,
79-80.

[37] Cf. Zimmerli, ibid., p. 49.

[38] Cf. Zimmerli, ibid., pp. 51, 65, 83.

[39] Cf. Zimmerli, ibid., pp. 113-16.

[40] Cf. Zimmerli, ibid., pp. 100-01.

[41] Cf. Zimmerli, ibid., pp. 88-98.

[42] Cf. Zimmerli, ibid., p. 103.

[43] On the importance of Ezek. 20 cf. Zimmerli, "Ich
bin Jahwe," pp. 18 ff., and Elliger, op. cit., pp. 225-
27. Zimmerli stresses the similarities (along with
some differences) between Ex. 6 and Ezek. 20. Elliger
emphasizes the situation of theophany as the original
setting for "I am Yahweh," and he also points out that
the self-predication is associated here with both grace
and law.

[44] Cf. note 42.

[45] Cf. especially W. Stewart McCullough, "Exegesis
of Psalms 72-92, 94, 97-99, 101-119, 139," The Interpreter's Bible (New York and Nashville: Abingdon Press,
1955), IV, p. 438, who points out that the word "feast"
in vs. 3 is used of all three annual festivals (Passover, Weeks, Tabernacles), but only the first day of
Passover and of Tabernacles approximates the middle of
the month ("full moon").

[46] Cf. Bernhard W. Anderson, Out of the Depths:
The Psalms Speak for Us Today (Philadelphia: The Westminster Press, 1983), p. 172.

[47] Cf. Harvey H. Guthrie, Jr., Israel's Sacred
Songs: A Study of Dominant Themes (New York: The Seabury
Press, 1966), pp. 29, 47-51.

[48] At the beginning of the psalm, Mitchell Dahood
would translate oz as "fortress," a name for the ark of
the covenant (cf. Ps. 78:61), and he would therefore
read "the God of our Fortress" rather than "God our
strength." Cf. Psalms II, 51-100, The Anchor Bible
(Garden City, New York: Doubleday & Company, Inc., 1968),

p. 263. This translation suggests that the psalm had
its setting at one of the cultic centers in which the
ark was prominent.

[49] On the so-called Elohistic Psalter (Pss. 42-83),
in which editors supposedly substituted elohim for
Yahweh, cf. William R. Taylor, "Exegesis of Psalms 1-
71, 93, 95-96, 100, 120-138, 140-150," The Interpreter's
Bible (New York and Nashville: Abingdon Press, 1955),
IV, p. 221.

[50] James Philip Hyatt regards chapter 24 in Jeremiah
as a literary product of Deuteronomic origin; cf.
"Introduction and Exegesis of Jeremiah," The Interpreter's Bible (New York and Nashville: Abingdon Press,
1956), V, pp. 996-98. With regard to vs. 7, however,
it should be noted that the formula "I am Yahweh" is
rare in Deuteronomy and the Deuteronomic corpus (Joshua
through Kings).

[51] The fact that after 587 B.C., Jeremiah was taken
to Egypt and spent the remainder of his life there does
not seem relevant in this connection; it was as a resi-
dent of Jerusalem that he employed the formula "I am
Yahweh."

[52] This figure excludes Ezek. 28:2 (el ani) and
28:9 (elohim ani), in which the prince of Tyre is
represented as claiming divinity for himself. The
figure also excludes the covenant formula "I will be
your (their) God." In Hebrew this is literally "I will
be to you (them) for God," i.e., it is a statement of
intention by God rather than a self-predication. For
this type of statement cf. Gen. 17:8; Ex. 6:7; 29:45;
Lev. 11:45; 26:12, 45; Num. 15:41; Jer. 7:23; 11:4;
24:7; 30:22; 31:1, 33; 32:38; Ezek. 11:20; 34:24;
36:28; 37:23, 27; Zech. 8:8.

[53] For similar statements in which a person claims
divinity for himself, cf. the boast of the prince of
Tyre, "I am a god" (Ezek. 28:2, 9), and the statement
by Pompey, "I will be lord of land and sea" (Ps. Sol.
2:33). For the use of ani alone in an everyday sense
to mean "I am he" or "I am the one," cf. II Sam. 20:17;
similarly, with anoki, I Sam. 4:16.

[54] Ps. 100:3 illustrates a pleonastic use of hu in
apposition with the subject: Yahweh hu elohim, "Yahweh,
he (is) God." For similar examples in the second
person, in which hu is used pleonastically in apposition

with a predicate noun, cf. II Sam. 7:28; Is. 37:16;
Ps. 44:4 (Heb. 44:5); Neh. 9:6, 7. These examples seem
to anticipate the later use of hu as the functional
equivalent of the linking verb; cf. Carl Brockelmann,
Grundriss der vergleichenden Grammatik der semitischen
Sprachen (Hildesheim: G. Olms, 1961), II, para. 52-53,
149b.

[55] Cf. Otto Eissfeldt, op. cit., pp. 226-27.

[56] Cf. G. Ernest Wright, "The Book of Deuteronomy,"
The Interpreter's Bible (New York and Nashville:
Abingdon-Cokesbury Press, 1953), II, pp. 515, 517.

[57] Cf. S.R. Driver, A Critical and Exegetical
Commentary on Deuteronomy, The International Critical
Commentary (New York: Charles Scribner's Sons, 1902),
pp. 345-48.

[58] Elsewhere the two verbs occur together only in
Ps. 30:2-3 (Heb. 30:3-4) and Ezek. 47:9.

[59] The only possible exception is Is. 45:15, which
is probably a comment by II Isaiah rather than a statement by the Israelite exiles.

[60] Ani Yahweh, Is. 41:4, 13; 42:6, 8; 43:3, 15;
45:3, 5, 6, 7, 18, 19; 48:17; 49:23, 26. Anoki Yahweh,
Is. 44:24; 51:15. Anoki anoki Yahweh, Is. 43:11.

[61] Ani eloheka, Is. 41:10. Ani el, Is. 43:12;
45:22. Anoki el, Is. 46:9.

[62] Ani hu, Is. 41:4; 43:10, 13; 46:4; 48:12; 52:6.
Anoki anoki hu, Is. 43:25; 51:12.

[63] On the background, structure, and function of
the salvation oracle, cf. Philip B. Harner, "The Salvation Oracle in Second Isaiah," Journal of Biblical
Literature 88 (1969), pp. 418-34. More recently, see
also M.H.E. Weippert, "De herkomst van het heilsorakel
voor Israël bij Deutero-Jesaja," Nederlands Theologisch
Tijdschrift 36 (Jan. 1982), pp. 1-11. According to
Weippert, the salvation oracle in II Isaiah represents
a redirecting of the "royal oracle" (a form of speech
attested in both Assyrian and Old Testament texts) from
the Davidic king to the people of Israel.

[64] For the idea of "holiness," cf. Norman H. Snaith,
The Distinctive Ideas of the Old Testament (London: The
Epworth Press, 1944), pp. 21-50.

65 Form-critically, Is. 44:6-8 may be regarded as a "mixed" passage combining elements from the hymn of self-praise, the trial scene between Yahweh and other gods, and the salvation oracle.

66 Cf. Hugo Gressmann, op. cit., pp. 254-97, especially p. 290. It should be noted, however, that Gressmann did not differentiate between this "hymnic expansion" and the salvation oracle.

67 H.-M. Dion, "Le genre littéraire sumérien de l' 'Hymne à soi-même' et quelques passages du Deutéro-Isaïe," Revue Biblique 74 (1967), pp. 215-34; the quotation is from p. 215.

68 Ibid., pp. 219-20, 222, 227, 230-31.

69 On the expression "in secret," cf. James Muilenburg, op. cit., p. 532, who believes that the phrase refers to secret mysteries, symbolism, oracles, or knowledge available only within a cultic group, in contrast to Yahweh's word that is relevant to Israel's historical situation. For a different view cf. Claus Westermann, op. cit., p. 173, who believes that the reference is not to the mystery cults of other religions but to Israel's own belief that Yahweh's word through earlier prophets had led only to "darkness and nothingness."

70 Cf. Muilenburg, ibid.

71 On the words tsedeq and mesharim, cf. Ludwig Koehler and Walter Baumgartner, Lexicon in Veteris Testamenti Libros (Leiden: E.J. Brill, 1958), pp. 520, 794-95.

72 Cf. Joachim Begrich, Studien zu Deuterojesaja, Theologische Bücherei, Altes Testament, 20 (München: Chr. Kaiser Verlag, 1963), pp. 48, 52.

73 Cf. Claus Westermann, Sprache und Struktur der Prophetie Deuterojesajas, Calwer Theologische Monographien, 11 (Stuttgart: Calwer Verlag, 1981), pp. 47, 49-51.

74 Cf. above, section III.A.5.

75 On the covenant formula cf. above, note 52.

[76] Cf. John L. McKenzie, S.J., op. cit., p. 40.

[77] Cf. Claus Westermann, Isaiah 50-66, pp. 29, 101.

[78] Cf. John L. McKenzie, S.J., op. cit., pp. xxxix-xlii.

[79] Cf. James Muilenburg, op. cit., pp. 406-14, especially pp. 407-08. Cf. also Arvid S. Kapelrud, Et folk på hjemferd: "Trøsteprofeten" -- den annen Jesaja -- og hans budskap (Oslo: Universitetsforlaget, 1964), pp. 50-86. With regard to the theory (which goes back to Bernhard Duhm) that the Servant poems were added later by someone else, Kapelrud notes (p. 53) that this would mean that two religious geniuses left their mark on Is. 40-55, and he suggests that this would be very remarkable in a time that was "more than poor" in great personalities.

[80] Cf. James Muilenburg, op. cit., p. 466.

[81] Cf. W. Gesenius, E. Kautzsch, and A.E. Cowley, Gesenius' Hebrew Grammar, Second English Edition (Oxford: Clarendon Press, 1957), para. 116a (p. 356).

[82] Joachim Jeremias, The Sermon on the Mount (Philadelphia: Fortress Press, 1963), especially pp. 24-25.

BIBLIOGRAPHY OF REFERENCES CITED

Anderson, Bernhard W. Out of the Depths: The Psalms
    Speak for Us Today. Philadelphia: The Westminster
    Press, 1983.

Begrich, Joachim. Studien zu Deuterojesaja. Theolo-
    gische Bücherei, Altes Testament, 20. München:
    Chr. Kaiser Verlag, 1963.

Brockelmann, Carl. Grundriss der vergleichenden
    Grammatik der semitischen Sprachen. Hildesheim:
    G. Olms, 1961.

Childs, Brevard S. The Book of Exodus: a Critical,
    Theological Commentary. Philadelphia: The
    Westminster Press, 1974.

Dahood, Mitchell. Psalms II, 51-100. The Anchor Bible.
    Garden City, New York: Doubleday & Company, Inc.,
    1968.

Dion, H.-M. "Le genre littéraire sumérien de l' 'Hymne
    à soi-même' et quelques passages du Deutéro-Isaïe."
    Revue Biblique 74 (1967), pp. 215-34.

Driver, S.R. A Critical and Exegetical Commentary on
    Deuteronomy. The International Critical Commen-
    tary. New York: Charles Scribner's Sons, 1902.

Eichrodt, Walther. Theology of the Old Testament.
    Vol. I. London: SCM Press Ltd, 1961.

Eissfeldt, Otto. The Old Testament: An Introduction.
    New York and Evanston: Harper & Row, Publishers,
    1965.

Elliger, Karl. "Ich bin der Herr -- euer Gott." In
    Kleine Schriften zum Alten Testament. Theologische
    Bücherei 32. Pp. 211-31. München: Chr. Kaiser
    Verlag, 1966.

Gesenius, W., and E. Kautzsch and A.E. Cowley.
    Gesenius' Hebrew Grammar. Second English Edition.
    Oxford: Clarendon Press, 1957.

Gray, John. "Exodus." In The Interpreter's One-Volume
    Commentary on the Bible. Nashville & New York:
    Abingdon Press, 1971.

Gressmann, Hugo. "Die literarische Analyse Deutero-
    jesajas." Zeitschrift für die alttestamentliche
    Wissenschaft 34 (1914), pp. 254-97.

Guthrie, Harvey H., Jr. Israel's Sacred Songs: A Study
    of Dominant Themes. New York: The Seabury Press,
    1966.

Harner, Philip B. "The Salvation Oracle in Second
    Isaiah." Journal of Biblical Literature 88
    (1969), pp. 418-34.

Hillers, Delbert R. Covenant: The History of a Biblical
    Idea. Baltimore: The Johns Hopkins Press, 1969.

Hyatt, James Philip. "Introduction and Exegesis of
    Jeremiah." In The Interpreter's Bible, V. New
    York and Nashville: Abingdon Press, 1956.

Jeremias, Joachim. The Sermon on the Mount. Phila-
    delphia: Fortress Press, 1963.

Kapelrud, Arvid S. Et folk på hjemferd: "Trøstepro-
    feten" -- den annen Jesaja -- og hans budskap.
    Oslo: Universitetsforlaget, 1964.

Koehler, Ludwig, and Walter Baumgartner. Lexicon in
    Veteris Testamenti Libros. Leiden: E.J. Brill,
    1958.

Langdon, Stephen. Die neubabylonischen Königs-
    inschriften. Leipzig: J.C. Hinrichs, 1912.

McCullough, W. Stewart. "Exegesis of Psalms 72-92, 94,
    97-99, 101-119, 139." In The Interpreter's Bible,
    IV. New York and Nashville: Abingdon Press, 1955.

McKenzie, John L., S.J. Second Isaiah. The Anchor
    Bible, Vol. 20. Garden City, New York: Doubleday
    & Company, Inc., 1968.

Muilenburg, James. "The Book of Isaiah: Chapters 40-
    66." In The Interpreter's Bible, V. New York and
    Nashville: Abingdon Press, 1966.

Norden, Eduard. Agnostos Theos. Leipzig and Berlin:
    B.G. Teubner, 1923.

Pritchard, James B., ed. Ancient Near Eastern Texts
    Relating to the Old Testament. 2nd ed. Princeton:
    Princeton University Press, 1955.

Rogers, Robert William. Cuneiform Parallels to the Old
    Testament. New York: Eaton & Mains; Cincinnati:
    Jennings & Graham, 1912.

Snaith, Norman H. The Distinctive Ideas of the Old
    Testament. London: The Epworth Press, 1944.

Taylor, William R. "Exegesis of Psalms 1-71, 93,
    95-96, 100, 120-138, 140-150." In The Interpre-
    ter's Bible, IV. New York and Nashville: Abingdon
    Press, 1955.

Weippert, M.H.E. "De herkomst van het heilsorakel voor
    Israël bij Deutero-Jesaja." Nederlands Theologisch
    Tijdschrift 36 (Jan. 1982), pp. 1-11.

Westermann, Claus. Isaiah 40-66. The Old Testament
    Library. Philadelphia: The Westminster Press,
    1969.

Westermann, Claus. Sprache und Struktur der Prophetie
    Deuterojesajas. Calwer Theologische Monographien,
    Vol. 11. Stuttgart: Calwer Verlag, 1981.

Wright, G. Ernest. "The Book of Deuteronomy." In The
    Interpreter's Bible, II. New York and Nashville:
    Abingdon-Cokesbury Press, 1953.

Zimmerli, Walther. "Erkenntnis Gottes nach dem Buche
    Ezechiel." In Gottes Offenbarung: Gesammelte
    Aufsätze. Theologische Bücherei, Vol. 19.
    München: Chr. Kaiser Verlag, 1963.

Zimmerli, Walther. "Ich bin Jahwe." In Gottes Offen-
    barung: Gesammelte Aufsätze. Theologische
    Bücherei, Vol. 19. München: Chr. Kaiser Verlag,
    1963.

INDEX OF SCRIPTURAL REFERENCES

Romans
     3:24   166.
     6:1   166.
     6:4   166.
     6:11   167.

Galatians
     5:6   167.
     5:13-14   167.
     5:22-23   167.
     5:25   167.

Ephesians
     2:8   167.
     2:9   167.
     2:10   167.

I John
     4:11   167.
     4:19   167.

Ancient Near Eastern Texts and Studies